PHUKET TRAVEL GUIDE

2024

Discovering Paradise: A Comprehensive Guide to Phuket's Hidden Gems, Adventure, and Culture

DOMINIC POPE

Copyright © by Dominic Pope, 2024.

All rights reserved. No part of this publication may be reproduced, distributed, or transmitted in any form or by any means, including photocopying, recording, or other electronic or mechanical methods, without the prior written permission of the publisher, except in the case of brief quotations embodied in critical reviews and certain other noncommercial uses permitted by copyright law.

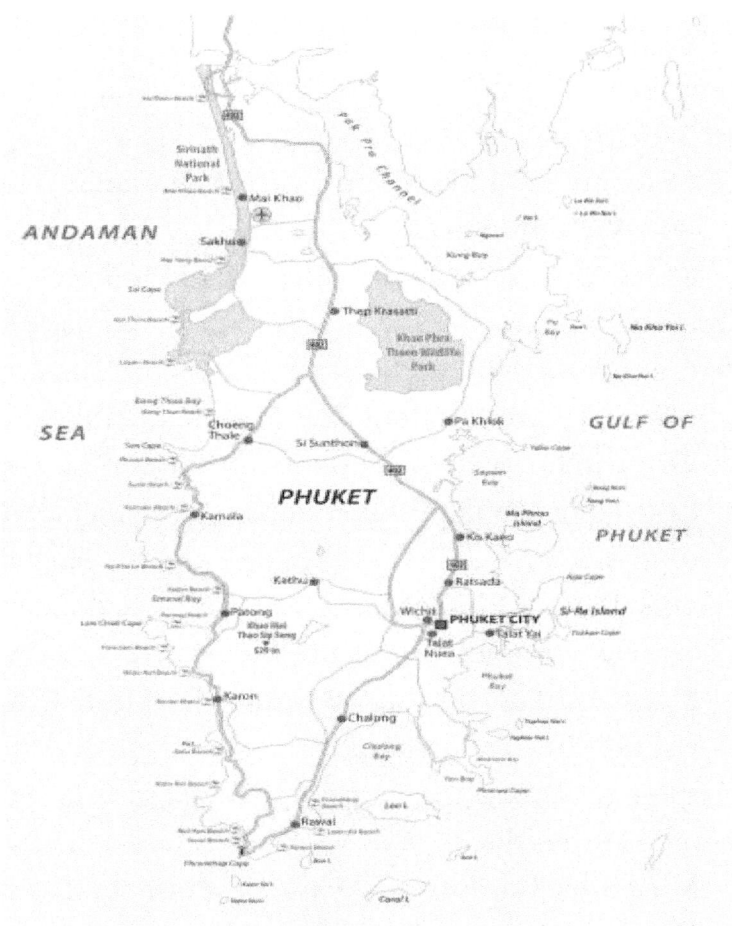

Map of Phuket

Table of Content

Chapter 1 1
Introduction 1
   Welcome to Phuket: The Jewel of Thailand 1
   Why Visit Phuket? 4
   Quick Tips for a Memorable Trip to Phuket 7

Chapter 2 11
Planning Your Trip to Phuket 11
   How to Get to Phuket 11
   Visa and Entry Requirements for Phuket 16
   Best Time to Visit Phuket 18

Chapter 3 23
Getting Around Phuket 23
   Transportation Options in Phuket 23
   Maps and Transportation Guides for Phuket .. 27
   Useful Phrases in Thai 30

Chapter 4 33
Iconic Landmarks 33
   Museums, Gardens and Parks in Phuket 33
   Best Neighborhood to visit in Phuket 40
   Top Attractions in Phuket 46
   Hidden Gems off the Beaten Path 56

Chapter 5 67
Experiencing the Culture and Cuisine 67
   Understanding Thai Culture and Etiquette 67
   Festivals and Celebrations in Phuket 70

 Traditional Thai Cuisine: Must-Try Dishes...... 73
 Dining Etiquette and Food Adventures........... 76
Chapter 6.. 81
Adventures in Nature... 81
 Island Hopping: Exploring Phuket's Surrounding Islands.. 81
 Jungle Treks and Wildlife Encounters............. 89
 Eco-Tourism and Sustainable Travel Tips........ 98
Chapter 7...103
Accommodation Options..................................... 103
 Choosing the Right Accommodation for Your Stay... 103
 Budget-Friendly Stays...................................... 106
 Luxury Resorts and Boutique Hotels...............110
 Unique Accommodation Experiences............. 114
Chapter 8.. 119
Nightlife and Entertainment................................ 119
 Phuket after Dark: Nightlife Hotspots............ 119
 Cultural Shows and Performances................. 123
 Evening Markets and Street Food Delights.... 126
Chapter 9.. 131
Shopping and Souvenirs....................................... 131
 Where to Shop in Phuket: Markets, Malls, and Boutiques.. 131
 Unique Souvenir Ideas.................................... 135
 Bargaining Tips for a Successful Shopping Experience.. 138

Chapter 10..141
Practical and Safety Tips............................141
    Money Matters: Currency, Tipping, and
    Bargaining...141
    Staying Safe in Phuket: Dos and Don'ts..........143
    Health and Medical Services............................147
    Emergency Contact Information....................149
Chapter 11..153
Itineraries...153
    1-week Itinerary..153
    Exciting Day Trips from Phuket......................156
    Exploring Nearby Islands................................161
    Adventure Activities beyond Phuket..............165
Conclusion..171

Chapter 1

Introduction

Welcome to Phuket: The Jewel of Thailand

Imagine stepping onto a land where azure waters gently kiss the shorelines of pristine beaches, where verdant jungles teem with exotic wildlife, and where vibrant culture dances in the streets under the warm tropical sun. Welcome to Phuket – the jewel of Thailand, a destination that promises a tapestry of experiences, adventures, and unforgettable memories waiting to be woven.

As you embark on your journey to Phuket, allow yourself to be enchanted by the allure of this island paradise. But before you set foot on its shores, let's take a moment to immerse ourselves in the essence of Phuket, to understand its rich tapestry of history, culture, and natural beauty.

A Glimpse into Phuket's Past

Phuket's history is as vibrant and colorful as its sunsets. Once a haven for pirates and traders navigating the Andaman Sea, Phuket has evolved into a melting pot of cultures, where Thai traditions intertwine with influences from China, India, and Europe. From the ancient sea gypsies who first settled its shores to the bustling trading port it became in the 19th century, Phuket's past whispers tales of resilience, adventure, and transformation.

Dive into Phuket's Diversity

Prepare to be captivated by Phuket's diverse landscapes and experiences. Whether you seek the pulsating energy of Patong's nightlife, the tranquil serenity of hidden beaches in Rawai, or the cultural treasures nestled in Phuket Town's narrow streets, there's something for every traveler's soul to discover. Explore limestone cliffs that plunge into emerald waters, dive into underwater worlds teeming with vibrant marine life, or trek through lush jungles echoing with the calls of exotic birds – Phuket invites you to embrace every moment with wonder and curiosity.

Embracing Thai Hospitality

At the heart of Phuket's allure lies the warmth and hospitality of its people. Prepare to be greeted with genuine smiles and gracious hospitality wherever you go. From savoring authentic Thai cuisine bursting with flavors to participating in age-old traditions and celebrations, immerse yourself in the vibrant tapestry of local life. Whether you're bargaining at a bustling market or learning the graceful movements of Thai dance, each interaction offers a glimpse into the soul of Phuket.

Practical Tips for a Seamless Journey

Before you embark on your adventure, arm yourself with practical knowledge to ensure a seamless journey. From understanding local customs and etiquette to navigating transportation options and staying safe, a little preparation goes a long way in maximizing your enjoyment of Phuket. Remember to respect the natural environment and cultural heritage of this beautiful island, leaving only footprints and taking home memories that will last a lifetime.

Embark on Your Phuket Adventure

Now that you've glimpsed into the essence of Phuket, it's time to embark on your own adventure. Whether you're seeking relaxation, adventure, or cultural immersion, Phuket promises an experience like no other. So pack your sense of wonder, leave your worries behind, and let Phuket weave its magic around you. Your journey begins here, in the jewel of Thailand – welcome to Phuket.

Why Visit Phuket?

Nestled in the embrace of the Andaman Sea, Phuket beckons travelers with its irresistible charm and boundless allure. From pristine beaches fringed with swaying palm trees to vibrant markets teeming with exotic treasures, Phuket offers a tapestry of experiences that captivate the senses and leave an indelible mark on the soul. Here are just a few reasons why Phuket should be at the top of your travel bucket list:

1. Breathtaking Beaches:

Phuket boasts some of the world's most stunning beaches, each with its own unique character and charm. Whether you're seeking the vibrant energy of Patong Beach, the tranquil serenity of Kata Noi, or the secluded paradise of Freedom Beach, there's a stretch of sand to suit every mood and preference.

2. Rich Cultural Heritage:

Immerse yourself in Phuket's rich cultural tapestry, where Thai traditions blend harmoniously with influences from China, India, and beyond. Explore ornate temples adorned with intricate carvings, witness vibrant festivals that light up the streets with color and music, and savor the flavors of authentic Thai cuisine passed down through generations.

3. Thrilling Adventures:

For adrenaline junkies and nature lovers alike, Phuket offers a playground of adventure waiting to be explored. Dive into crystal-clear waters teeming with colorful marine life, soar above lush jungles on a zip line, or embark on a trek through rugged terrain to discover hidden waterfalls and panoramic vistas.

4. Vibrant Nightlife:

As the sun sets, Phuket comes alive with an electrifying energy that pulses through its streets and venues. Whether you're sipping cocktails at a beachfront bar, dancing the night away at a bustling club, or taking in a traditional Thai performance, the island offers endless opportunities for nocturnal excitement and entertainment.

5. Island Hopping Excursions:

Venture beyond Phuket's shores and discover a world of natural wonders waiting to be explored. Embark on island-hopping excursions to nearby gems such as Phi Phi Islands, James Bond Island, and Similan Islands, where pristine beaches, azure waters, and breathtaking scenery await at every turn.

6. Wellness and Relaxation:

Indulge in ultimate relaxation and rejuvenation at Phuket's world-class spas and wellness retreats. From traditional Thai massages and holistic therapies to yoga sessions overlooking the ocean, Phuket offers a sanctuary for those seeking to nourish mind, body, and soul.

7. Warm Hospitality:

Above all, Phuket welcomes visitors with open arms and genuine hospitality that leaves a lasting impression. Whether you're exploring bustling markets, interacting with locals, or simply relaxing on the beach, you'll find yourself embraced by the warmth and friendliness of the Thai people.

In essence, Phuket offers a tantalizing blend of natural beauty, cultural richness, adventure, and relaxation that beckons travelers from around the globe. Whether you're seeking adventure, romance, or simply a moment of serenity, Phuket promises an unforgettable journey that will leave you longing to return again and again.

Quick Tips for a Memorable Trip to Phuket

Embarking on a journey to Phuket promises excitement, adventure, and unforgettable experiences. To ensure your trip is as smooth and enjoyable as possible, here are some quick tips to keep in mind:

1. Plan Ahead:

Take the time to research and plan your itinerary in advance. Consider factors such as the weather, local events, and attractions you don't want to miss. Booking accommodations and activities ahead of time can help you avoid last-minute hassles and ensure availability.

2. Respect Local Customs:

Phuket is steeped in rich cultural traditions, so it's important to respect local customs and etiquette. Dress modestly when visiting temples or religious sites, remove your shoes before entering someone's home or a sacred space, and always greet locals with a respectful "wai" (a slight bow with hands pressed together).

3. Stay Hydrated:

The tropical climate of Phuket can be hot and humid, so be sure to drink plenty of water throughout the day to stay hydrated. Carry a reusable water bottle with you and refill it regularly to avoid dehydration, especially if you're spending time outdoors or engaging in physical activities.

4. Protect Yourself from the Sun:

Don't let sunburn put a damper on your vacation. Apply sunscreen with a high SPF before heading outdoors, and reapply it regularly, especially after swimming or sweating. Wearing a wide-brimmed hat, sunglasses, and lightweight clothing can also help shield your skin from the sun's harmful rays.

5. Practice Safe Swimming:

While Phuket's beaches are undeniably beautiful, it's important to exercise caution when swimming in the ocean. Pay attention to warning flags and signage indicating hazardous conditions, and always swim in designated areas supervised by lifeguards. Be mindful of strong currents, waves, and potential marine hazards such as jellyfish or sea urchins.

6. Sample Local Cuisine:

One of the highlights of any trip to Phuket is indulging in its tantalizing culinary delights. Don't be afraid to venture beyond familiar dishes and sample authentic Thai cuisine at local eateries and street food stalls. Be adventurous and try dishes like pad Thai, green curry, tom yum soup, and mango sticky rice for a true taste of Thailand.

7. Bargain Wisely:

Bargaining is a common practice at markets and street vendors in Phuket, but remember to do so respectfully and with a smile. Start by offering a lower price than the initial asking price and be prepared to negotiate until you reach a mutually agreeable amount. Keep in mind that haggling is part of the local culture, so have fun with it!

8. Stay Safe and Aware:

While Phuket is generally a safe destination for travelers, it's important to stay vigilant and aware of your surroundings. Keep your belongings secure, especially in crowded areas or tourist hotspots, and avoid walking alone in unfamiliar or poorly lit areas at night. Trust your instincts and exercise caution, just as you would in any unfamiliar environment.

By keeping these quick tips in mind, you'll be well-equipped to embark on a memorable and rewarding journey to Phuket. Whether you're seeking relaxation, adventure, or cultural immersion, this tropical paradise promises an experience like no other. Safe travels, and may your time in Phuket be filled with joy, discovery, and unforgettable moments.

Chapter 2

Planning Your Trip to Phuket

How to Get to Phuket

Phuket, the gem of the Andaman Sea, is a tropical paradise accessible by various modes of transportation. Whether you're arriving from within Thailand or traveling from abroad, here are the most common ways to get to Phuket:

1. By Air:

Phuket International Airport (HKT) is the main gateway to the island and serves both domestic and international flights. Numerous airlines operate direct flights to Phuket from major cities around the world, including Bangkok, Singapore, Hong Kong, Kuala Lumpur, and more. Upon arrival at Phuket International Airport, travelers can easily access the island's beaches and attractions via taxi, airport shuttle, or rental car.

2. By Bus:

Traveling to Phuket by bus is a budget-friendly option for those exploring Thailand from within the country. Phuket Bus Terminal 2, located in Phuket Town, serves as the main bus terminal for long-distance buses arriving from cities such as Bangkok, Krabi, Surat Thani, and other provinces in southern Thailand. Several bus companies offer both standard and VIP bus services with varying levels of comfort and amenities.

3. By Train and Bus Combination:

While Phuket does not have its own railway station, travelers can take a train to nearby provinces such as Surat Thani or Trang and then transfer to a bus for the remainder of the journey to Phuket. This option provides a scenic route through the Thai countryside and is popular among travelers seeking a more adventurous and immersive experience.

4. By Ferry:

For those traveling from nearby islands or coastal provinces, ferries offer a convenient and scenic way to reach Phuket. Ferry services operate regularly from destinations such as Phi Phi Islands, Krabi, Koh Lanta, and Ao Nang, with multiple departure points and companies to choose from. Travelers can opt for high-speed ferries for a quicker journey or traditional long-tail boats for a more leisurely cruise.

5. By Car:

Travelers driving to Phuket from other parts of Thailand can take advantage of well-maintained highways and road networks that connect the island to major cities such as Bangkok, Krabi, and Phang Nga. The journey to Phuket by car offers flexibility and the opportunity to explore scenic routes and attractions along the way. Rental car services are available at airports and in major cities, providing travelers with the freedom to explore Phuket at their own pace.

No matter which mode of transportation you choose, arriving in Phuket is just the beginning of an unforgettable journey filled with sun-drenched beaches, lush landscapes, vibrant culture, and endless adventures awaiting exploration. Whether you're arriving by air, land, or sea, let the beauty and warmth of Phuket welcome you with open arms.

Visa and Entry Requirements for Phuket

Before embarking on your journey to Phuket, it's essential to familiarize yourself with the visa and entry requirements to ensure a smooth and hassle-free arrival. Here's what you need to know:

1. Visa Exemption:

Citizens of many countries are eligible for visa exemption when traveling to Thailand for tourism purposes. Visitors from countries such as the United States, Canada, the United Kingdom, Australia, and most European nations can enter Thailand without a visa for stays of up to 30 days. However, it's essential to check the latest regulations as they may vary depending on your nationality.

2. Visa on Arrival:

For travelers who are not eligible for visa exemption, Thailand offers a visa on arrival option at major international airports and land border crossings. This allows visitors to obtain a tourist visa upon arrival, typically valid for stays of up to 15 or 30 days, depending on the country of origin. Be sure to have the necessary documentation, including a passport with at least six months validity, proof of onward travel, and sufficient funds for your stay.

3. Tourist Visa:

If you plan to stay in Thailand for longer than the visa exemption or visa on arrival allows, you may need to apply for a tourist visa in advance at a Thai embassy or consulate in your home country. Tourist visas are typically valid for stays of up to 60 days and may be extendable for an additional 30 days within Thailand.

4. Departure Requirements:

When departing from Phuket, ensure that you have all necessary documentation, including a valid passport and any required exit visas or departure taxes. Additionally, be prepared to undergo security and health screenings at the airport before boarding your flight.

5. Electronic Visa Application:

Some travelers may be eligible to apply for an electronic visa (eVisa) or visa waiver through Thailand's online visa application system. This streamlined process allows for the convenient online submission of visa applications, reducing the need for in-person visits to embassies or consulates.

6. Travel Insurance:

While not a visa requirement, it's highly recommended to purchase travel insurance before your trip to Phuket. Travel insurance can provide coverage for medical emergencies, trip cancellations, lost or stolen belongings, and other unforeseen circumstances, offering peace of mind during your travels.

By familiarizing yourself with these visa and entry requirements before your trip to Phuket, you can ensure a smooth and hassle-free arrival, allowing you to focus on enjoying all that this tropical paradise has to offer.

Best Time to Visit Phuket

Phuket, with its tropical climate and stunning natural beauty, offers visitors a slice of paradise year-round. However, certain times of the year are more favorable for specific activities or weather preferences. Here's a breakdown of the best times to visit Phuket based on weather, crowds, and seasonal events:

1. High Season (November to March):

- **Weather:** The high season in Phuket brings cooler temperatures, lower humidity, and clear skies, making it ideal for beach activities and outdoor adventures. Daytime temperatures hover around the mid-80s Fahrenheit (around 30°C), with little to no rainfall.

- **Crowds:** As one of the peak tourist seasons, expect larger crowds and higher prices for accommodations and attractions, especially around Christmas and New Year. Booking in advance is recommended.

- **Events:** November marks the beginning of the Phuket high season, with events such as Loy Krathong (the Thai Festival of Lights) and the King's Cup Regatta attracting visitors from around the world.

2. Shoulder Season (April to May):

- **Weather:** April and May in Phuket bring rising temperatures and humidity levels, with occasional brief showers or thunderstorms. While still warm and sunny, it's advisable to seek shade and stay hydrated during outdoor activities.

- **Crowds:** Crowds begin to taper off after the high season, offering a more relaxed atmosphere and potentially better deals on accommodations and tours. However, popular beaches and attractions may still see moderate crowds, especially during holidays and festivals.

- **Events:** Songkran, the Thai New Year festival celebrated in mid-April, brings water fights and festive activities to the streets of Phuket, making it a lively time to visit.

3. Low Season (June to October):

- **Weather:** The low season in Phuket is characterized by higher temperatures, increased humidity, and the possibility of heavy rainfall and occasional storms, particularly from June to September. However, rain showers are typically short-lived and followed by sunshine.

- **Crowds:** With fewer tourists visiting during the low season, you'll find quieter beaches, discounted hotel rates, and more space to explore popular attractions without the crowds.

- **Events:** While fewer events take place during the low season, travelers can still enjoy cultural festivals such as the Por Tor Festival in August, which honors ancestral spirits with colorful ceremonies and vegetarian feasts.

4. Best Time for Specific Activities:

- **Diving and Snorkeling:** The best time for diving and snorkeling in Phuket is during the high season (November to March) when underwater visibility is excellent, and sea conditions are calm.

- **Surfing:** Surfers flock to Phuket's west coast beaches from May to October, when the southwest monsoon brings larger waves and ideal surfing conditions.

- **Whale Watching:** From November to February, visitors can embark on whale watching tours to spot migrating humpback whales passing through the Andaman Sea.

Ultimately, the best time to visit Phuket depends on your preferences, whether you prioritize weather conditions, crowd levels, or specific activities. Regardless of when you choose to visit, Phuket's natural beauty and warm hospitality await, promising an unforgettable experience in this tropical paradise.

Chapter 3

Getting Around Phuket

Transportation Options in Phuket

Exploring Phuket and its surrounding areas is made convenient with a variety of transportation options catering to different preferences and budgets. Here's a guide to getting around Phuket:

1. Tuk-Tuks:

- **Description:** Tuk-tuks are iconic three-wheeled motorized taxis that offer a fun and adventurous way to navigate Phuket's streets.

- **Availability:** Tuk-tuks can be found throughout Phuket, especially in tourist areas like Patong, Kata, and Karon Beach.

- **Fare:** Fares are usually negotiable, so be prepared to haggle for the best price before starting your journey.

- **Best For:** Short distances and quick trips within town, as well as experiencing a quintessential Thai mode of transportation.

2. **Taxis:**

- **Description:** Metered taxis and private taxis are widely available in Phuket and offer a comfortable and convenient way to travel.

- **Availability:** Metered taxis can be hailed from designated taxi stands, while private taxis can be arranged through hotels or booked in advance.

- **Fare:** Metered taxis charge based on distance and time, while private taxis may have fixed rates or negotiated fares.

- **Best For:** Longer distances, airport transfers, and exploring attractions beyond the reach of tuk-tuks.

3. **Motorbike Taxis:**

- **Description:** Motorbike taxis, recognizable by their brightly colored vests, are a fast and efficient way to navigate through traffic.

- **Availability:** Motorbike taxi stands are commonly found along main roads and in busy areas, offering quick rides to nearby destinations.

- **Fare:** Fares are usually negotiated upfront and tend to be cheaper than traditional taxis, especially for short trips.

- **Best For:** Short-distance travel, avoiding traffic congestion, and exploring narrow or crowded streets.

4. Rental Cars and Motorbikes:

- **Description:** Renting a car or motorbike provides the ultimate freedom to explore Phuket at your own pace and convenience.

- **Availability:** Rental agencies are plentiful in tourist areas and at Phuket International Airport, offering a range of vehicles to suit different needs and budgets.

- **Fare:** Rental prices vary depending on the type of vehicle, rental duration, and insurance coverage.

- **Best For:** Exploring remote areas, scenic drives, and day trips to nearby attractions with flexibility and independence.

5. Songthaews:

- **Description:** Songthaews are shared pickup trucks with bench seating in the back, serving as a cost-effective mode of transportation.

- **Availability:** Songthaews operate along established routes and can be flagged down or boarded at designated stops.

- **Fare:** Fares are usually fixed based on the distance traveled and are often lower than other forms of public transportation.

- **Best For:** Getting around town and traveling between different areas of Phuket on a budget.

6. Public Buses:

- **Description:** Phuket's public bus system offers an affordable way to travel between major towns and attractions on the island.

- **Availability:** Buses operate on scheduled routes, with stops at key locations such as Phuket Town, Patong, Kata, and Karon.

- **Fare:** Fares are fixed and inexpensive, making public buses a budget-friendly option for getting around Phuket.

- **Best For:** Traveling between towns, visiting attractions along established routes, and experiencing local life.

No matter which transportation option you choose, getting around Phuket is relatively straightforward, allowing you to explore the island's diverse landscapes, attractions, and hidden gems with ease. Consider your itinerary, budget, and preferences when selecting the best mode of transportation for your Phuket adventure.

Maps and Transportation Guides for Phuket

Navigating Phuket's diverse landscapes and attractions is made easier with the help of maps and transportation guides designed to assist travelers in getting around the island efficiently. Here's how you can access and utilize maps and transportation guides to enhance your Phuket experience:

1. Online Maps and Apps:

- **Description:** Utilize online mapping services and mobile apps such as Google Maps, Apple Maps, or Maps.me to navigate Phuket's roads and landmarks with ease.

- **Features:** These digital maps offer real-time navigation, traffic updates, and points of interest, allowing you to plan routes, find nearby attractions, and discover hidden gems.

- **Accessibility:** Accessible on smartphones, tablets, and computers, online maps provide convenient navigation tools for travelers exploring Phuket on foot, by car, or via public transportation.

2. Printed Maps:

- **Description:** Pick up printed maps and transportation guides from hotels, tourist information centers, or car rental agencies upon arrival in Phuket.

- **Features:** Printed maps typically highlight major roads, attractions, beaches, and points of interest, providing an overview of Phuket's geography and key destinations.

- **Convenience:** Keep a printed map on hand for easy reference when exploring Phuket's streets, especially in areas with limited internet connectivity or GPS signal.

3. Hotel Concierge Services:

- **Description:** Seek assistance from your hotel's concierge desk or front desk staff for recommendations on transportation options, routes, and attractions.

- **Services:** Hotel concierge services can provide customized transportation guides, arrange taxi or shuttle services, and offer insider tips on getting around Phuket efficiently.

- **Local Knowledge:** Take advantage of the local expertise and insights offered by hotel staff to enhance your travel experience and discover hidden gems off the beaten path.

4. Transportation Apps and Services:

- **Description:** Download transportation apps such as Grab, Uber (if available), or local ride-hailing services to book taxis, tuk-tuks, or private drivers in Phuket.

- **Convenience:** These apps offer convenient booking, fare estimation, and payment options, allowing you to arrange transportation on the go without the need for cash or language proficiency.

- **Safety:** Choose reputable transportation providers with positive reviews and ratings to ensure safe and reliable journeys around Phuket.

5. Local Tourist Information Centers:

- **Description:** Visit local tourist information centers located in Phuket Town or popular tourist areas for maps, brochures, and transportation guides.

- **Assistance:** Knowledgeable staff at tourist information centers can provide personalized recommendations, answer questions about transportation options, and offer guidance on planning your itinerary.

- **Additional Services:** Some tourist information centers may offer bike rentals, guided tours, or transportation packages for exploring Phuket's attractions with ease.

By utilizing maps and transportation guides, whether digital or printed, you can navigate Phuket's streets, beaches, and attractions with confidence and ease. Whether you're embarking on a self-guided adventure or seeking assistance from local resources, these tools are invaluable companions for exploring all that Phuket has to offer.

Useful Phrases in Thai

Learning a few useful phrases in Thai can greatly enhance your experience while traveling in Phuket and interacting with locals. Here are some essential phrases to help you navigate everyday situations with ease:

1. Hello / Goodbye:

- Sawasdee (สวัสดี) - Hello / Goodbye (formal)

- Bai-bai (บายบาย) - Goodbye (informal)

2. Thank You:

- Khob khun (ขอบคุณ) - Thank you

- Khob khun khrap (ขอบคุณครับ) - Thank you (male speaker)

- Khob khun kha (ขอบคุณค่ะ) - Thank you (female speaker)

3. Yes / No:

- Chai (ใช่) - Yes

- Mai chai (ไม่ใช่) - No

4. Please:

- Khrap (ครับ) - Please (male speaker)

- Kha (ค่ะ) - Please (female speaker)

5. Excuse Me / Sorry:

- Khaw thot (ขอโทษ) - Excuse me / Sorry

6. How Much?:

- Tao rai (เท่าไหร่) - How much?

7. Where is...?:

- Yoo tee nai (อยู่ที่ไหน) - Where is...?

8. I Don't Understand:

- Mai khao jai (ไม่เข้าใจ) - I don't understand

9. Do You Speak English?

- Kun phoot pasa angkrit dai mai (คุณพูดภาษาอังกฤษได้ไหม) - Do you speak English?

10. Can You Help Me?

- Chuay chan dai mai (ช่วยฉันได้ไหม) - Can you help me?

11. I'm Lost:

- Chan tham nai (ฉันหลงทาง) - I'm lost

12. Delicious / Tasty:

- Aroi (อร่อย) - Delicious / Tasty

13. Bathroom / Toilet:

- Hong nam (ห้องน้ำ) - Bathroom / Toilet

14. Water:

- Nam (น้ำ) - Water

15. Cheers!

- Chok dee (โชคดี) - Cheers!

Remember to speak slowly and clearly when using these phrases, and don't be afraid to gesture or use simple drawings to help convey your message if needed. Locals appreciate the effort, and even a few basic phrases can go a long way in fostering positive interactions and building connections during your time in Phuket.

Chapter 4

Iconic Landmarks

Museums, Gardens and Parks in Phuket

While Phuket is renowned for its stunning beaches and vibrant nightlife, the island also boasts a variety of museums, gardens, and parks that offer insight into its rich history, culture, and natural beauty. Here are some noteworthy attractions to explore beyond the shoreline:

1. Phuket Thai Hua Museum:

- **Description:** Housed in a beautifully restored Sino-Portuguese building in Phuket Town, the Thai Hua Museum offers a fascinating glimpse into Phuket's Chinese heritage and cultural identity. Exhibits include displays on immigration, tin mining, local festivals, and traditional customs.

- **Location:** Krabi Road, Talat Yai, Mueang Phuket District, Phuket Town

2. Phuket Trickeye Museum:

- **Description:** This interactive museum features mind-bending 3D artwork that allows visitors to become part of the exhibits through creative photo opportunities. With optical illusions and immersive paintings, the Trickeye Museum offers a fun and entertaining experience for all ages.

- **Location:** 130/1 Phangnga Rd, Tambon Talat Yai, Mueang Phuket District, Phuket Town

3. Thalang National Museum:

- **Description:** Situated near the Heroines' Monument, the Thalang National Museum showcases artifacts, exhibits, and historical information related to Phuket's cultural heritage and early settlements. Learn about the island's indigenous peoples, the impact of tin mining, and key events in its history.

- **Location:** Si Sunthon, Thalang District, Phuket

4. Phuket Mining Museum:

- **Description:** Located in Kathu, the Phuket Mining Museum offers insight into the island's tin mining industry, which played a significant role in its development. Exhibits include mining equipment, dioramas depicting life in the mines, and multimedia presentations detailing the history of tin extraction.

- **Location:** 26/5 Moo 5, Kathu District, Phuket

5. Phuket Botanic Garden:

- **Description:** Escape the hustle and bustle of the city at the Phuket Botanic Garden, a tranquil oasis showcasing a diverse collection of tropical plants, orchids, and exotic flora from around the world. Stroll through themed gardens, admire water features, and enjoy panoramic views of the surrounding hills.

- **Location:** 98/89 Moo 4, Tambon Chalong, Mueang Phuket District, Phuket

6. Sirinat National Park (Nai Yang Beach):

- **Description:** Sirinat National Park, encompassing Nai Yang Beach and Mai Khao Beach, offers pristine natural beauty, lush coastal vegetation, and important nesting grounds for sea turtles. Explore walking trails, relax on the beach, and keep an eye out for wildlife such as monitor lizards and migratory birds.

- **Location:** Thalang District, Phuket

7. Khao Phra Thaeo National Park:

- **Description:** Covering a vast area of rainforest and hills in northern Phuket, Khao Phra Thaeo National Park is a haven for nature lovers and outdoor enthusiasts. Trekking trails lead to scenic viewpoints, waterfalls, and the park's namesake temple, Wat Phra Thaeo, which houses a revered Buddha image.

- **Location:** Thep Krasattri, Thalang District, Phuket

Exploring these museums, gardens, and parks in Phuket offers a deeper understanding of the island's cultural heritage, natural environment, and hidden gems beyond its famous beaches. Whether you're seeking cultural immersion, family-friendly activities, or serene moments in nature, these attractions provide enriching experiences for travelers of all interests.

Best Neighborhood to visit in Phuket

Phuket is a diverse island with a variety of neighborhoods, each offering its own unique charm, attractions, and atmosphere. While the "best" neighborhood to visit in Phuket ultimately depends on your interests and preferences, here are a few standout areas that are popular among visitors:

1. Patong Beach:

- **Description:** As one of the liveliest and most vibrant areas in Phuket, Patong Beach is renowned for its bustling nightlife, vibrant street markets, and wide range of entertainment options. From beachfront bars and restaurants to shopping malls and nightclubs, Patong offers non-stop excitement for those seeking a lively atmosphere.

- **Highlights:** Bangla Road (famous for its nightlife), Jungceylon Shopping Mall, Patong Beach, Simon Cabaret Show

2. Phuket Old Town:

- **Description:** Steeped in history and culture, Phuket Old Town boasts charming Sino-Portuguese architecture, colorful colonial buildings, and a laid-back ambiance. Stroll along narrow streets lined with boutique shops, art galleries, and quaint cafes, and admire the well-preserved heritage buildings that reflect Phuket's multicultural heritage.

- **Highlights:** Thalang Road, Soi Romanee, Phuket Thai Hua Museum, Sunday Walking Street Market

3. Kata Beach:

- **Description:** Kata Beach offers a more relaxed and family-friendly atmosphere compared to bustling Patong. With soft white sands, clear turquoise waters, and picturesque surroundings, Kata Beach is perfect for swimming, sunbathing, and water sports such as surfing and snorkeling. The area also boasts a range of dining options and beachfront resorts.

- **Highlights:** Kata Viewpoint, Kata Noi Beach, Kata Night Market, Surf House Phuket

4. Kamala Beach:

- **Description:** Nestled between Patong and Surin Beach, Kamala Beach offers a tranquil and laid-back alternative to the more crowded tourist areas. This charming fishing village boasts a beautiful crescent-shaped beach, local markets, and a relaxed atmosphere ideal for couples and families seeking a peaceful retreat.

- **Highlights:** Phuket FantaSea Cultural Theme Park, Kamala Friday Night Market, Kamala Beach

5. Surin Beach:

- **Description:** Known as the "Millionaire's Row" due to its upscale resorts and luxury villas, Surin Beach exudes an air of sophistication and exclusivity. With powdery white sands, crystal-clear waters, and swaying palm trees, Surin Beach offers a serene and picturesque setting for sunbathing, swimming, and enjoying upscale dining and shopping options.

- **Highlights:** Catch Beach Club, Surin Plaza, Laem Singh Viewpoint, Twinpalms Phuket Resort

6. Rawai Beach:

- **Description:** Located on the southeastern coast of Phuket, Rawai Beach is a laid-back area known for its local seafood restaurants, authentic Thai markets, and traditional longtail boat tours to nearby islands. Rawai offers a glimpse into everyday life in Phuket and serves as a gateway to nearby attractions such as Promthep Cape and Coral Island.

- **Highlights:** Sea Gypsy Village, Rawai Beach Pier, Rawai Park, Laem Promthep (Promthep Cape)

Whether you're seeking vibrant nightlife, cultural immersion, family-friendly activities, or tranquil beach retreats, Phuket's diverse neighborhoods offer something for every traveler's taste and preference. Explore these distinct areas to discover the unique charms and hidden gems that make Phuket a beloved destination for visitors from around the world.

Top Attractions in Phuket

Phuket is a treasure trove of attractions, offering something for every type of traveler, whether you're seeking adventure, relaxation, cultural experiences, or natural beauty. Here are some of the top attractions that you shouldn't miss when visiting Phuket:

1. Patong Beach:

- **Description:** One of the most famous beaches in Phuket, Patong Beach is known for its vibrant atmosphere, soft sands, and crystal-clear waters. It's also the epicenter of nightlife in Phuket, with an array of bars, restaurants, and nightclubs along Bangla Road.

2. Phi Phi Islands:

- **Description:** Just a boat ride away from Phuket, the Phi Phi Islands are renowned for their breathtaking scenery, pristine beaches, and crystal-clear waters ideal for snorkeling and diving. Don't miss iconic spots like Maya Bay and Monkey Beach.

3. Big Buddha:

- **Description:** Sitting atop Nakkerd Hill, the Big Buddha is a towering 45-meter-tall statue that offers panoramic views of Phuket. It's a sacred site for locals and visitors alike, providing a peaceful atmosphere for meditation and reflection.

4. Phang Nga Bay and James Bond Island:

- **Description:** Explore the stunning limestone karsts and emerald-green waters of Phang Nga Bay, famously featured in the James Bond movie "The Man with the Golden Gun." Take a boat tour to James Bond Island and enjoy kayaking through sea caves and mangrove forests.

5. Wat Chalong:

- **Description:** As one of the most important Buddhist temples in Phuket, Wat Chalong is a beautiful complex adorned with intricate architecture, statues, and shrines. Visitors can explore the temple grounds, learn about Buddhist teachings, and pay respects to revered relics.

6. Phuket Old Town:

- **Description:** Wander through the charming streets of Phuket Old Town, where colorful Sino-Portuguese buildings, quaint cafes, and boutique shops line the historic streets. Don't miss the Sunday Walking Street Market for local crafts, street food, and live performances.

7. Simon Cabaret Show:

- **Description:** Experience the glitz and glamour of Phuket's famous cabaret show, featuring dazzling performances by talented transgender artists in elaborate costumes and sets. The Simon Cabaret Show promises an unforgettable evening of entertainment and spectacle.

8. Kata Noi Beach:

- **Description:** Tucked away from the crowds, Kata Noi Beach offers a tranquil retreat with soft sands, clear waters, and stunning views of the Andaman Sea. It's perfect for sunbathing, swimming, and enjoying water sports in a more peaceful setting.

9. Phuket Elephant Sanctuary:

- **Description:** Visit the Phuket Elephant Sanctuary for a responsible and ethical elephant encounter. Learn about these magnificent animals, observe them in their natural habitat, and participate in feeding and bathing activities while supporting their welfare and conservation.

10. Bangla Road, Patong:

- **Description:** Experience the vibrant nightlife of Phuket at Bangla Road in Patong, where neon lights, live music, street performers, and lively bars and clubs create an electrifying atmosphere after dark.

These top attractions in Phuket offer a taste of the island's diverse offerings, from stunning natural landscapes to cultural landmarks and thrilling entertainment. Whether you're exploring the beaches, temples, or vibrant streets, Phuket promises an unforgettable journey filled with adventure, beauty, and relaxation.

Hidden Gems off the Beaten Path

Exploring the hidden gems of Phuket off the beaten path can reveal secluded beaches, serene viewpoints, cultural treasures, and unique experiences away from the crowds. Here are some hidden gems worth discovering during your visit to Phuket:

1. Freedom Beach:

- **Description:** Tucked away from the hustle and bustle of Patong, Freedom Beach offers a secluded paradise with powdery white sands, turquoise waters, and lush greenery. Accessible by boat or a short hike through the jungle, this hidden gem is perfect for a peaceful day of sunbathing and swimming.

2. Ao Sane Beach:

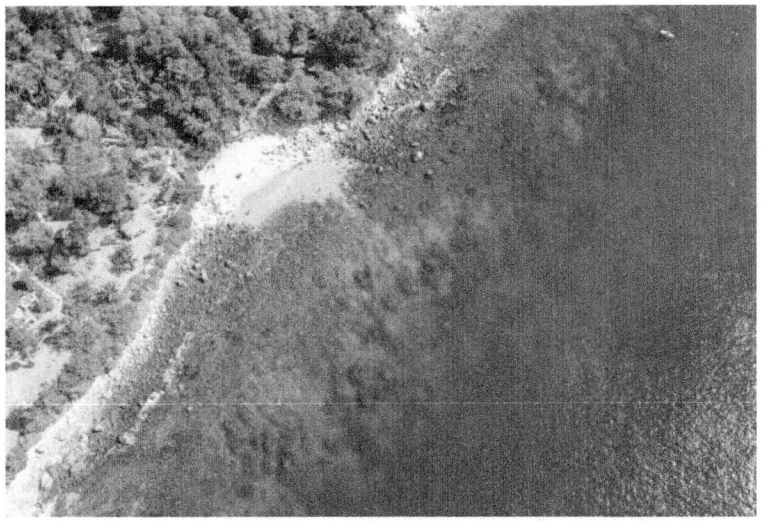

- **Description:** Located near Nai Harn Beach, Ao Sane Beach is a hidden cove surrounded by rocky cliffs and coral reefs. This tranquil spot is popular among snorkelers and divers for its vibrant marine life and crystal-clear waters. Facilities are limited, adding to its untouched charm.

3. Khao Rang Viewpoint:

- **Description:** Escape the crowds and enjoy panoramic views of Phuket Town from Khao Rang Viewpoint. Located on a hilltop, this hidden gem offers stunning vistas of the cityscape, lush hillsides, and distant islands. Relax at the viewpoint's hilltop park and enjoy a meal at the nearby restaurant.

4. Laem Singh Viewpoint:

- **Description:** For a lesser-known alternative to popular viewpoints like Promthep Cape, head to Laem Singh Viewpoint in Phuket's southwest. This hidden gem offers breathtaking vistas of the Andaman Sea, with fewer visitors and a more peaceful atmosphere. It's perfect for watching the sunset in tranquility.

5. Coconut Island (Koh Maphrao):

- **Description:** Escape to the idyllic Coconut Island, just a short boat ride from Phuket's east coast. This hidden gem boasts secluded beaches, lush coconut groves, and a laid-back atmosphere ideal for relaxation and exploration. Rent a kayak or bicycle to discover the island's hidden corners.

6. Khao Phra Thaeo Wildlife Sanctuary:

- **Description:** Explore the untouched beauty of Phuket's largest protected area, Khao Phra Thaeo Wildlife Sanctuary. This hidden gem is home to pristine rainforests, waterfalls, and diverse wildlife, including gibbons and rare bird species. Hike along nature trails and enjoy the serenity of nature.

7. Bang Pae Waterfall:

- **Description:** Discover the tranquil oasis of Bang Pae Waterfall hidden within Khao Phra Thaeo Wildlife Sanctuary. Follow a short jungle trail to reach this picturesque cascade, where you can cool off in natural pools and enjoy the lush surroundings away from the crowds.

8. Ban Teelanka (The UpsideDown House Phuket):

- **Description:** Experience a unique attraction at Ban Teelanka, also known as The UpsideDown House Phuket. This quirky museum features a fully furnished house built entirely upside down, offering interactive exhibits and photo opportunities that defy gravity and spark imagination.

9. Sirinat National Park:

- **Description:** Escape to the tranquility of Sirinat National Park, a hidden gem encompassing pristine beaches, mangrove forests, and important sea turtle nesting grounds. Explore walking trails, relax on secluded stretches of sand, and enjoy birdwatching and nature photography.

10. Nai Thon Beach:

- **Description:** Experience the untouched beauty of Nai Thon Beach, a hidden gem on Phuket's northwest coast. With soft sands, turquoise waters, and lush vegetation, this secluded bay offers a peaceful retreat away from the crowds, perfect for swimming, snorkeling, and picnicking.

These hidden gems off the beaten path in Phuket offer unique opportunities for exploration, relaxation, and discovery, allowing you to uncover the island's natural beauty and cultural treasures beyond its popular tourist attractions. Whether you're seeking secluded beaches, serene viewpoints, or off-the-grid adventures, Phuket has hidden gems waiting to be explored.

Chapter 5

Experiencing the Culture and Cuisine

Understanding Thai Culture and Etiquette

Understanding Thai culture and etiquette is essential for visitors to Phuket to ensure respectful interactions and meaningful experiences during their stay. Here are some key aspects of Thai culture and etiquette to keep in mind:

1. Respect for the Monarchy:

- Thais hold deep reverence for the monarchy, and any criticism or disrespect toward the royal family is considered highly offensive and may be punishable by law. Avoid discussing sensitive political topics related to the monarchy.

2. Wai Greeting:

- The traditional Thai greeting, known as the wai, involves placing your palms together in a prayer-like gesture with a slight bow. The wai is used to show respect and gratitude when greeting others, especially elders or those in positions of authority.

3. Modest Dress:

- When visiting temples, religious sites, or local communities, dress modestly and avoid revealing clothing. Cover your shoulders, chest, and knees as a sign of respect for Thai culture and religious customs.

4. Removing Shoes:

- It is customary to remove your shoes before entering temples, homes, and certain businesses, as shoes are considered unclean. Look for a shoe rack or follow the lead of locals to determine when to remove your shoes.

5. Politeness and Saving Face:

- Thais value politeness, harmony, and avoiding confrontation. Maintain a calm and respectful demeanor in all interactions, and avoid raising your voice or displaying anger, as this may cause embarrassment or loss of face for both parties.

6. Public Displays of Affection:

- Public displays of affection, such as kissing or hugging, are generally not common or culturally appropriate in Thai society. Show restraint and avoid overly affectionate behavior in public settings.

7. Buddhist Customs and Practices:

- Buddhism plays a significant role in Thai culture, and visitors should be mindful of Buddhist customs and practices. Show respect when visiting temples, observe silence and remove hats and sunglasses within temple grounds, and refrain from touching or pointing at sacred objects or statues.

8. Tolerance and Acceptance:

- Thais are known for their tolerant and accepting attitude toward different cultures and beliefs. Embrace diversity and be open to learning about Thai customs, traditions, and ways of life.

9. Generosity and Sharing:

- Thai culture places importance on generosity and sharing, whether it's offering food to monks, giving alms to the less fortunate, or participating in community events and festivals. Be generous with your time, resources, and kindness during your travels in Phuket.

10. Bargaining:

- Bargaining is common in markets and street stalls in Thailand, but it should be done respectfully and with a smile. Start with a friendly negotiation and be willing to compromise to reach a fair price for goods or services.

By understanding and respecting Thai culture and etiquette, visitors can foster positive interactions, build meaningful connections, and create memorable experiences during their time in Phuket. Embrace the warmth, hospitality, and rich traditions of Thai culture, and you'll be welcomed with open arms by the people of Phuket.

Festivals and Celebrations in Phuket

Phuket is renowned for its vibrant festivals and celebrations, which showcase the island's rich cultural heritage, religious traditions, and lively spirit. Here are some of the most notable festivals and celebrations in Phuket:

1. Vegetarian Festival (Tesagan Gin Je):

- **Description:** Held annually in Phuket Town and other Chinese-Thai communities across the island, the Vegetarian Festival is a nine-day event celebrated by the Chinese-Thai community during the ninth lunar month of the Chinese calendar. Participants observe strict vegetarian diets and engage in various rituals, including spirit possession, firewalking, and piercing rituals.

- **Date:** Usually in September or October

2. Songkran (Thai New Year):

- **Description:** Songkran is the traditional Thai New Year celebration, marked by water fights, street parties, and religious ceremonies. Locals and visitors alike participate in the joyful festivities by splashing water on each other as a symbol of cleansing and renewal. It's one of the most lively and colorful events in Phuket.

- **Date:** April 13-15

3. Phuket Old Town Festival:

- **Description:** This annual festival celebrates the rich history, culture, and heritage of Phuket's Old Town area. Visitors can enjoy street performances, cultural displays, traditional music and dance, local cuisine, and art exhibitions. The festival highlights the unique charm and architectural beauty of Phuket's historic district.

- **Date:** Usually in February

4. Loy Krathong (Festival of Lights):

- **Description:** Loy Krathong is a nationwide festival celebrated throughout Thailand, including Phuket, to pay respects to the water spirits and seek forgiveness for past misdeeds. Participants release decorated floats (krathongs) onto bodies of water, such as rivers, lakes, and the sea, accompanied by prayers and wishes for good fortune.

- **Date:** Usually in November

5. Phuket Bike Week:

- **Description:** Phuket Bike Week is an annual gathering of motorcycle enthusiasts from around the world, featuring motorcycle rallies, parades, live music performances, bike exhibitions, and parties. Riders explore scenic routes around the island and participate in charity rides and community events.

- **Date:** Usually in April

6. Chao Le (Sea Gypsy) Boat Floating Festival:

- **Description:** The Chao Le Boat Floating Festival is a traditional ceremony observed by the sea gypsy community in Phuket to honor their ancestors and pay respects to the sea. Elaborately decorated boats are launched into the water, accompanied by rituals, prayers, and cultural performances.

- Date: **Usually in March**

7. Phuket Gay Pride Festival:

- **Description:** Phuket Gay Pride is a colorful and inclusive celebration of LGBTQ+ pride, diversity, and equality. The festival features parades, beach parties, drag shows, cultural events, and community activities that promote acceptance and solidarity within the LGBTQ+ community and beyond.

- **Date:** Usually in April

8. Thao Thep Krasattri and Thao Si Sunthon Fair:

- **Description:** This annual fair honors Thao Thep Krasattri and Thao Si Sunthon, two legendary sisters who played a crucial role in defending Phuket from Burmese invaders in the 18th century. The fair features cultural performances, traditional games, food stalls, and historical reenactments.

- **Date:** Usually in March

These festivals and celebrations offer visitors a unique opportunity to immerse themselves in Phuket's vibrant culture, traditions, and community spirit. Whether you're participating in religious rituals, enjoying street festivities, or savoring local cuisine, these events showcase the diverse and colorful tapestry of life in Phuket.

Traditional Thai Cuisine: Must-Try Dishes

Traditional Thai cuisine is renowned for its bold flavors, aromatic herbs, and vibrant colors. Here are some must-try dishes that exemplify the rich culinary heritage of Thailand:

1. Pad Thai:

- **Description:** Pad Thai is one of Thailand's most iconic dishes, featuring stir-fried rice noodles with eggs, tofu, shrimp, or chicken, flavored with tamarind, fish sauce, garlic, chilies, and palm sugar. It's commonly served with bean sprouts, chopped peanuts, lime wedges, and fresh herbs.

2. Tom Yum Goong:

- **Description:** Tom Yum Goong is a hot and sour soup made with fragrant lemongrass, kaffir lime leaves, galangal, chili peppers, and lime juice, simmered with shrimp, mushrooms, and other seafood. It's known for its bold and refreshing flavors, with a perfect balance of spicy, sour, and savory elements.

3. Green Curry (Gaeng Keow Wan):

- **Description:** Green Curry is a classic Thai curry made with green chili paste, coconut milk, Thai eggplant, bamboo shoots, and your choice of meat (such as chicken, beef, or pork). It's aromatic, creamy, and slightly sweet, with a hint of heat from the green chilies.

4. Som Tum (Papaya Salad):

- **Description:** Som Tum is a refreshing and spicy salad made with shredded green papaya, tomatoes, green beans, peanuts, and chili peppers, dressed with lime juice, fish sauce, garlic, and palm sugar. It's a perfect balance of flavors, with a crunchy texture and a kick of heat.

5. Massaman Curry:

- **Description:** Massaman Curry is a rich and fragrant curry with influences from Persian and Indian cuisine, featuring tender chunks of meat (such as beef or chicken), potatoes, onions, and peanuts, simmered in a creamy coconut milk-based sauce flavored with spices like cinnamon, cardamom, and star anise.

6. Pad Kra Pao (Basil Chicken):

- **Description:** Pad Kra Pao is a popular stir-fry dish made with minced chicken or pork, stir-fried with garlic, Thai chilies, holy basil, and soy sauce, served over rice and topped with a fried egg. It's savory, aromatic, and packed with bold flavors.

7. Mango Sticky Rice (Khao Niew Mamuang):

- **Description:** Mango Sticky Rice is a beloved Thai dessert made with ripe mangoes, sticky rice soaked in coconut milk, and topped with a drizzle of coconut cream and toasted sesame seeds. It's a delightful combination of sweet, creamy, and fragrant flavors.

8. Gaeng Daeng (Red Curry):

- **Description:** Red Curry is another classic Thai curry made with red chili paste, coconut milk, vegetables, and your choice of meat or tofu. It's slightly spicier than green curry and has a rich, creamy texture that pairs perfectly with steamed rice.

9. Pad See Ew:

- **Description:** Pad See Ew is a comforting stir-fried noodle dish made with wide rice noodles, Chinese broccoli, eggs, and your choice of meat (such as chicken, beef, or shrimp), flavored with soy sauce, garlic, and a hint of sweetness.

10. Gaeng Kiew Wan Gai (Thai Green Chicken Curry):

- **Description:** Thai Green Chicken Curry is a fragrant and flavorful curry made with green curry paste, coconut milk, chicken, Thai eggplant, bamboo shoots, and kaffir lime leaves. It's aromatic, slightly spicy, and bursting with Thai herbs and spices.

These traditional Thai dishes offer a tantalizing journey through the diverse flavors and culinary traditions of Thailand, showcasing the country's love for fresh ingredients, aromatic herbs, and bold spices. Whether you're dining at a street food stall, a local restaurant, or a fine dining establishment, these must-try dishes promise a memorable gastronomic experience in Phuket.

Dining Etiquette and Food Adventures

Exploring dining etiquette and food adventures in Phuket can be a delightful journey into Thai culture and cuisine. Here are some tips for dining etiquette and food adventures to enhance your culinary experiences in Phuket:

Dining Etiquette:

1. The Wai:

- **Description:** When entering a restaurant or interacting with restaurant staff, a simple wai (placing palms together in a prayer-like gesture) is a polite way to show respect.

- **Usage:** Use the wai when greeting servers or expressing gratitude for their service.

2. Removing Shoes:

- **Description:** In some traditional Thai restaurants, you may be required to remove your shoes before entering. Look for a shoe rack or follow the lead of locals.

- **Usage:** Take off your shoes before stepping inside and place them neatly by the entrance.

3. Sharing Dishes:

- **Description:** Thai meals are often shared family-style, with several dishes ordered and enjoyed by everyone at the table.

- **Usage:** Don't be afraid to try a variety of dishes and share with your dining companions. It's customary to take small portions from communal dishes.

4. Chopsticks and Utensils:

- **Description:** While chopsticks are commonly used for noodle dishes, Thai cuisine typically uses a spoon and fork for most meals.

- **Usage:** Use the fork to push food onto the spoon, which is then used for eating. Chopsticks may be provided for specific dishes like noodle soups.

5. **Tasting Etiquette:**

- **Description:** It's polite to taste a small portion of each dish before adding condiments or seasonings.

- **Usage:** Take a small sample of each dish with your spoon to appreciate the flavors and adjust seasoning if necessary.

Food Adventures:

1. **Street Food Exploration:**

- **Description:** Wander through Phuket's vibrant street food markets to discover a diverse array of flavors, from savory noodles and grilled skewers to sweet treats and tropical fruits.

- **Experience:** Try local favorites like pad Thai, grilled seafood, mango sticky rice, and coconut ice cream from street vendors and night markets.

2. **Cooking Classes:**

- **Description:** Join a Thai cooking class to learn the art of Thai cuisine from expert chefs. Classes often include visits to local markets to select fresh ingredients.

- **Experience:** Participate in hands-on cooking sessions to prepare classic dishes such as green curry, tom yum soup, and spicy papaya salad, then savor your creations.

3. Seafood Feasts:

- **Description:** Indulge in a seafood feast at one of Phuket's many beachfront restaurants, where you can feast on freshly caught fish, prawns, crabs, and shellfish.

- **Experience:** Choose your seafood from a display of fresh catches and have it prepared to your liking, whether grilled, steamed, or stir-fried with aromatic herbs and spices.

4. Beachfront Dining:

- **Description:** Enjoy a romantic dinner or sunset cocktails at one of Phuket's beachfront restaurants, offering stunning views of the Andaman Sea and cool ocean breezes.

- **Experience:** Dine on fresh seafood, Thai specialties, and international cuisine while watching the sun sink below the horizon, creating a magical backdrop for your meal.

5. Local Markets and Food Tours:

- Description: Explore Phuket's bustling markets and embark on food tours to sample a variety of local delicacies and street food specialties.

- Experience: Join guided tours to navigate through food stalls, tasting authentic dishes, snacks, and desserts while learning about the culinary traditions of Thailand.

By embracing dining etiquette and embarking on food adventures in Phuket, you'll not only savor the delicious flavors of Thai cuisine but also gain insight into the rich culture and culinary heritage of the region. From street food exploration to beachfront dining experiences, Phuket offers a world of culinary delights waiting to be discovered.

Chapter 6

Adventures in Nature

Island Hopping: Exploring Phuket's Surrounding Islands

Island hopping around Phuket's surrounding islands is a popular activity that allows visitors to explore the stunning natural beauty, pristine beaches, and crystal-clear waters of the Andaman Sea. Here's a guide to island hopping adventures from Phuket:

1. Phi Phi Islands:

- **Description:** The Phi Phi Islands, including Phi Phi Don and Phi Phi Leh, are among the most famous destinations for island hopping from Phuket. Known for their breathtaking limestone cliffs, turquoise lagoons, and vibrant marine life, these islands offer opportunities for snorkeling, diving, and beach relaxation.

- **Highlights:** Maya Bay (featured in the movie "The Beach"), Monkey Beach, snorkeling at Loh Samah Bay, Viking Cave, and Phi Phi Viewpoint.

2. Similan Islands:

- **Description:** The Similan Islands are a group of nine granite islands renowned for their pristine beaches, coral reefs, and underwater biodiversity. The islands are part of a national marine park and offer some of the best diving and snorkeling sites in Thailand.

- **Highlights:** Richelieu Rock (a top dive site), Donald Duck Bay, Elephant Head Rock, and hiking trails on islands like Koh Similan and Koh Miang.

3. James Bond Island (Khao Phing Kan):

- **Description:** Made famous by its appearance in the James Bond movie "The Man with the Golden Gun," James Bond Island is a dramatic limestone rock formation rising from the sea. Visitors can explore the island's caves, beaches, and nearby attractions on organized boat tours.

- **Highlights:** Koh Tapu (James Bond Island), Koh Panyee (floating Muslim fishing village), sea kayaking through limestone caves, and scenic views of Phang Nga Bay.

4. Racha Islands (Racha Yai and Racha Noi):

- **Description:** The Racha Islands, also known as Raya Islands, offer pristine white-sand beaches, clear waters, and excellent snorkeling and diving opportunities. Racha Yai is the larger and more developed island, while Racha Noi is quieter and less visited.

- **Highlights:** Patok Beach and Siam Bay on Racha Yai, Ao Siam and Banana Bay on Racha Noi, snorkeling at Kon Kae Bay, and diving at sites like Marla's Mystery and South Tip.

5. Coral Island (Koh Hae):

- **Description:** Coral Island is a popular day trip destination from Phuket, known for its vibrant coral reefs, clear waters, and water sports activities. Visitors can enjoy snorkeling, diving, banana boat rides, parasailing, and relaxing on pristine beaches.

- **Highlights:** Long Beach and Banana Beach for sunbathing and water sports, snorkeling at Coral Island Reef, and exploring the island's interior on hiking trails.

6. Koh Yao Islands (Koh Yao Yai and Koh Yao Noi):

- **Description:** The Koh Yao Islands offer a serene and authentic alternative to the bustling tourist destinations of Phuket. These islands are known for their tranquil atmosphere, lush mangrove forests, and traditional fishing villages.

- **Highlights:** Yao Yai Beach, Loh Paret Beach, Chong Lad Pier for island hopping tours, kayaking through mangrove forests, and cultural experiences in local villages.

7. Koh Bon:

- **Description:** Koh Bon is a small island located north of the Similan Islands, known for its pristine dive sites and opportunities to encounter manta rays. It's a favorite destination for experienced divers looking for thrilling underwater adventures.

- **Highlights:** Manta Ray Point, Koh Bon Pinnacle, and Koh Bon West Ridge for encounters with manta rays and other marine life.

8. Koh Hae (Coral Island):

- **Description:** Coral Island, also known as Koh Hae, is a popular day trip destination from Phuket known for its clear waters and vibrant marine life. Visitors can enjoy activities such as snorkeling, scuba diving, banana boat rides, and parasailing.

- **Highlights:** Long Beach and Banana Beach for sunbathing and water sports, snorkeling at Coral Island Reef, and exploring the island's interior on hiking trails.

Tips for Island Hopping:

- **Choose a Reputable Tour Operator:** Select a trusted tour operator with good reviews and safety standards.

- **Pack Essentials:** Bring sunscreen, a hat, sunglasses, swimwear, a towel, and waterproof bags for valuables.

- **Respect Marine Life:** Practice responsible snorkeling and diving by avoiding touching or disturbing coral reefs and marine animals.

- **Stay Hydrated:** Bring plenty of water to stay hydrated, especially in the tropical heat.

- **Be Mindful of Seasickness:** If prone to seasickness, consider taking motion sickness medication before boarding the boat.

Island hopping from Phuket offers an incredible opportunity to explore the natural wonders and pristine beauty of Thailand's islands. Whether you're seeking adventure, relaxation, or underwater exploration, there's a destination for every traveler to discover in the Andaman Sea.

Jungle Treks and Wildlife Encounters

Exploring jungle treks and wildlife encounters in Phuket offers adventurers the chance to immerse themselves in the island's lush rainforests, discover hidden waterfalls, and encounter diverse flora and fauna. Here's a guide to jungle treks and wildlife encounters in Phuket:

1. Khao Phra Thaeo National Park:

- **Description:** Khao Phra Thaeo National Park is Phuket's largest protected area, covering lush rainforests, rugged hills, and diverse ecosystems. The park is home to various hiking trails, waterfalls, and wildlife, including macaques, gibbons, and rare bird species.

- **Highlights:** Bang Pae Waterfall, Ton Sai Waterfall, hiking trails to Khao Phra Thaeo viewpoint, and wildlife spotting along nature trails.

2. Elephant Sanctuaries:

- **Description:** Several ethical elephant sanctuaries in Phuket offer visitors the chance to observe and interact with rescued elephants in a natural environment. These sanctuaries promote responsible tourism and ethical elephant encounters, focusing on conservation and animal welfare.

- **Highlights:** Elephant feeding and bathing experiences, learning about elephant behavior and conservation efforts, and supporting ethical tourism practices.

3. Gibbon Rehabilitation Project:

- **Description:** The Gibbon Rehabilitation Project is dedicated to rescuing and rehabilitating gibbons that have been kept as pets or used for entertainment. Visitors can learn about the rehabilitation process, observe gibbons in semi-wild enclosures, and support conservation efforts.

- **Highlights:** Guided tours of the rehabilitation center, educational programs on gibbon conservation, and observing gibbons in their natural habitat.

4. Phuket Butterfly Garden and Insect World:

- **Description:** Phuket Butterfly Garden and Insect World is a tropical garden showcasing a variety of butterfly species, as well as exotic insects and reptiles. Visitors can explore lush gardens, butterfly habitats, and educational exhibits on insect conservation.

- **Highlights:** Butterfly gardens with colorful species, insect displays, educational programs on insect life cycles and habitats, and interactive exhibits for all ages.

5. Phuket Bird Paradise:

- **Description:** Phuket Bird Paradise is a sanctuary for tropical birds, housing a diverse collection of colorful species from around the world. Visitors can stroll through aviaries, observe birds in naturalistic habitats, and learn about bird conservation efforts.

- **Highlights:** Aviaries housing exotic bird species, interactive feeding sessions, educational programs on bird behavior and conservation, and opportunities for birdwatching and photography.

6. Jungle Zipline Adventures:

- **Description:** Jungle zipline adventures in Phuket offer adrenaline-pumping experiences as you soar through the rainforest canopy on zip lines and canopy bridges. These eco-friendly tours provide aerial views of the jungle and opportunities to spot wildlife from above.

- **Highlights:** Ziplining through lush rainforest canopy, crossing canopy bridges, guided tours with knowledgeable instructors, and learning about local flora and fauna.

7. Bang Pae Gibbon Rehabilitation Centre:

- **Description:** Located within Khao Phra Thaeo National Park, the Bang Pae Gibbon Rehabilitation Centre is dedicated to rescuing and rehabilitating gibbons that have been orphaned or injured. Visitors can learn about gibbon conservation efforts and observe these fascinating primates in a semi-wild environment.

- **Highlights:** Guided tours of the rehabilitation center, educational programs on gibbon behavior and conservation, and opportunities to support gibbon rehabilitation efforts through donations.

Tips for Jungle Treks and Wildlife Encounters:

- **Respect Wildlife:** Observe wildlife from a distance and avoid feeding or approaching animals.

- **Stay on Designated Trails:** Stick to marked trails to minimize impact on the environment and avoid getting lost.

- **Pack Essentials:** Bring water, snacks, insect repellent, sunscreen, and appropriate footwear for hiking.

- **Follow Park Regulations:** Adhere to park rules and regulations to protect the environment and wildlife.

- **Support Ethical Tourism:** Choose responsible tour operators and attractions that prioritize animal welfare and conservation.

Exploring jungle treks and wildlife encounters in Phuket offers an opportunity to connect with nature, discover hidden gems, and gain a deeper appreciation for the island's biodiversity and conservation efforts. Whether you're hiking through lush rainforests, observing wildlife in their natural habitat, or supporting ethical wildlife sanctuaries, Phuket promises unforgettable adventures for nature lovers and outdoor enthusiasts.

Eco-Tourism and Sustainable Travel Tips

Engaging in eco-tourism and practicing sustainable travel habits in Phuket can help minimize environmental impact and support local conservation efforts. Here are some eco-friendly travel tips for sustainable exploration in Phuket:

1. Choose Eco-Friendly Accommodations:

   - Opt for eco-friendly hotels, resorts, or guesthouses that prioritize sustainability practices, such as energy efficiency, waste reduction, water conservation, and use of renewable resources.

   - Look for eco-certifications or green initiatives implemented by accommodations, such as LEED certification, eco-friendly building materials, and recycling programs.

2. Support Responsible Tour Operators:

   - Select tour operators and activities that prioritize environmental conservation, wildlife protection, and responsible tourism practices.

   - Choose eco-friendly tours, such as nature walks, wildlife watching, snorkeling or diving excursions that support local conservation efforts and minimize environmental impact.

3. Reduce Plastic Usage:

- Bring a reusable water bottle and refill it at water stations or filtered water sources to avoid single-use plastic bottles.

- Say no to plastic straws, bags, and utensils, and carry a reusable shopping bag or tote for souvenirs and groceries.

4. Conserve Water and Energy:

- Take shorter showers, turn off lights, air conditioning, and electronics when not in use, and conserve water by reusing towels and linens.

- Choose accommodations and businesses that implement water-saving measures, such as low-flow faucets, toilets, and showerheads.

5. Respect Wildlife and Marine Life:

- Observe wildlife from a distance and avoid touching, feeding, or disrupting animals in their natural habitat.

- Practice responsible snorkeling and diving by avoiding contact with coral reefs, marine life, and underwater ecosystems, and never feed fish or marine animals.

6. Support Local Conservation Initiatives:

- Contribute to local conservation efforts by visiting national parks, wildlife sanctuaries, and protected areas that rely on visitor fees to fund conservation projects and habitat restoration.

- Participate in volunteer opportunities, community clean-up events, or wildlife monitoring programs organized by local conservation organizations.

7. Minimize Carbon Footprint:

- Choose eco-friendly transportation options, such as walking, cycling, or using public transportation, to explore Phuket and reduce carbon emissions.

- Consider carbon offsetting options for flights or travel activities to mitigate the environmental impact of your journey.

8. Respect Local Culture and Communities:

- Learn about and respect local customs, traditions, and cultural heritage, and support indigenous communities and artisans by purchasing locally made crafts and products.

- Engage in cultural exchange experiences, such as cooking classes, traditional performances, or homestay accommodations, to immerse yourself in the local way of life and support community-based tourism initiatives.

9. Leave No Trace:

- Practice Leave No Trace principles by packing out all waste, including trash, litter, and recyclables, and leaving natural areas as you found them.

- Dispose of waste responsibly in designated bins or recycling facilities and avoid littering or damaging sensitive ecosystems.

By adopting eco-friendly travel practices and supporting sustainable initiatives, you can minimize your environmental footprint, protect natural resources, and contribute to the preservation of Phuket's pristine landscapes and biodiversity for future generations to enjoy.

Chapter 7

Accommodation Options

Choosing the Right Accommodation for Your Stay

Choosing the right accommodation for your stay in Phuket can greatly enhance your overall travel experience. Here are some factors to consider when selecting accommodation options:

1. Location:

- Decide on the preferred location based on your travel preferences. Whether you prefer a beachfront resort, a quiet retreat in the hills, or a bustling area close to nightlife and attractions, choose a location that suits your needs and interests.

2. Budget:

- Determine your budget for accommodation and explore options within your price range. Phuket offers a wide range of accommodation choices, from budget-friendly guesthouses and hostels to luxury resorts and private villas.

3. Amenities and Facilities:

- Consider the amenities and facilities offered by the accommodation, such as swimming pools, fitness centers, spa services, restaurants, bars, and recreational activities. Choose accommodations that provide the amenities you desire for a comfortable and enjoyable stay.

4. Accommodation Type:

- Choose the type of accommodation that best suits your preferences and travel style, whether it's a hotel, resort, guesthouse, hostel, vacation rental, or boutique accommodation. Each type offers different levels of comfort, privacy, and services.

5. Safety and Security:

- Prioritize safety and security when choosing accommodation, especially if traveling solo or with family. Look for accommodations with secure locks,

24-hour reception or security, well-lit areas, and safety features such as fire extinguishers and smoke detectors.

6. Accessibility and Transportation:

- Consider accessibility and transportation options when choosing accommodation, including proximity to airports, public transportation, attractions, beaches, restaurants, and shopping areas. Choose a location with convenient access to the places you plan to visit.

7. Unique Experiences:

- Look for accommodations that offer unique experiences or special features, such as cultural activities, cooking classes, guided tours, eco-friendly initiatives, or wellness programs. These experiences can add value to your stay and create lasting memories.

8. Flexible Booking Policies:

- Check the accommodation's booking policies regarding cancellations, modifications, and refund options, especially if your travel plans may change. Look for accommodations with flexible booking policies to accommodate unforeseen circumstances.

9. Local Recommendations:

- Seek recommendations from locals, friends, or travel forums for hidden gems or off-the-beaten-path accommodations that may not be listed on popular booking websites. Local insights can help you discover unique and authentic places to stay.

By considering these factors and doing thorough research, you can choose the right accommodation for your stay in Phuket that meets your needs, preferences, and budget, ensuring a memorable and comfortable experience during your travels.

Budget-Friendly Stays

Here's a list of budget-friendly stays in Phuket:

1. Patong Backpacker Hostel

   - Located in the heart of Patong Beach

   - Offers dormitory-style accommodation

   - Budget-friendly rates with basic amenities

   - Close to nightlife, shopping, and dining options

2. Baan Laimai Beach Resort

   - Budget-friendly beachfront resort in Patong

   - Offers comfortable rooms with modern amenities

   - Features swimming pools, restaurants, and beach access

   - Close to Patong's attractions and entertainment venues

3. Kata Sea Breeze Resort

- Affordable resort located in Kata Beach area
- Offers cozy rooms with private balconies
- Features swimming pools, fitness center, and restaurant
- Short walk to Kata Beach and nearby restaurants

4. iHost Patong

- Budget-friendly guesthouse in Patong
- Offers clean and comfortable rooms with air conditioning
- Convenient location close to Patong Beach and Bangla Road
- Affordable rates with friendly staff

5. Pineapple Guesthouse

- Located in Phuket Town
- Offers budget-friendly accommodation with private bathrooms
- Close to local markets, restaurants, and attractions
- Ideal for travelers looking to explore Phuket Town's cultural sites

6. The Blue Pearl Kata Hotel

- Affordable hotel located in Kata Beach area

- Offers modern rooms with essential amenities

- Features swimming pool, restaurant, and tour desk

- Short walk to Kata Beach and Kata Night Market

7. Lub d Phuket Patong

- Budget-friendly hostel in Patong

- Offers dormitory-style and private rooms

- Features rooftop swimming pool, bar, and common areas

- Close to Patong Beach, Bangla Road, and Jungceylon Mall

8. Fulfil Phuket Hostel

- Located in Phuket Old Town

- Offers budget-friendly dormitory and private rooms

- Clean and comfortable accommodation with basic amenities

- Close to local cafes, restaurants, and historical sites

9. The Memory at On On Hotel

- Budget-friendly boutique hotel in Phuket Old Town

- Offers affordable rooms with heritage charm

- Features communal areas, library, and tour desk

   - Ideal for travelers interested in exploring Phuket's cultural heritage

10. Kata Bai D Inn

   - Affordable guesthouse in Kata Beach area

   - Offers simple rooms with essential amenities

   - Close to Kata Beach, restaurants, and shops

   - Suitable for budget-conscious travelers looking for a convenient location

These budget-friendly stays in Phuket offer comfortable accommodation options at affordable rates, allowing travelers to explore the island's attractions, beaches, and cultural sites without breaking the bank.

Luxury Resorts and Boutique Hotels

Here's a list of luxury resorts and boutique hotels in Phuket:

Luxury Resorts:

1. The Nai Harn Phuket

   - Located on Nai Harn Beach

   - Offers luxurious rooms and suites with ocean views

   - Features infinity pool, spa, fitness center, and multiple dining options

   - Known for its elegant design and personalized service

2. Trisara Phuket

- Exclusive luxury resort in a private bay

- Offers spacious villas and suites with private pools

- Features beachfront dining, spa, water sports, and yacht charters

- Known for its tranquil ambiance and breathtaking views

3. Banyan Tree Phuket

- Award-winning luxury resort in Bang Tao Bay

- Offers luxurious villas with private pools and lagoon views

- Features spa, golf course, dining options, and cultural experiences

- Known for its tropical gardens and serene atmosphere

4. Amanpuri

- Iconic luxury resort overlooking the Andaman Sea

- Offers elegant pavilions and villas with private pools

- Features beach club, spa, fitness center, and gourmet dining

- Known for its understated luxury and impeccable service

5. Sri Panwa Phuket Luxury Pool Villa Hotel

- Luxury resort perched on Cape Panwa

- Offers spacious villas with infinity pools and ocean views

- Features multiple dining options, spa, beach club, and water sports

- Known for its panoramic vistas and stylish design

Boutique Hotels:

1. The Slate

- Boutique hotel inspired by Phuket's tin mining heritage

- Offers unique rooms and suites with industrial-chic design

- Features swimming pools, spa, dining options, and cultural activities

- Known for its artistic flair and immersive experiences

2. Keemala

- Unique boutique resort nestled in the lush rainforest

- Offers luxurious villas inspired by different mythical clans

- Features spa, dining options, wellness activities, and nature trails

- Known for its innovative design and eco-friendly practices

3. The Shore at Katathani

- Intimate boutique hotel overlooking Kata Noi Beach

- Offers spacious pool villas with stunning sea views

- Features infinity pool, spa, dining options, and personalized service

- Known for its romantic ambiance and secluded location

4. Twinpalms Phuket

- Stylish boutique hotel in Surin Beach

- Offers contemporary rooms and suites with private terraces

- Features beach club, spa, dining options, and rooftop bar

- Known for its modern design and vibrant atmosphere

5. The Racha

- Boutique resort on Racha Island

- Offers luxurious villas and suites with sea views

- Features spa, dining options, water sports, and beach activities

- Known for its pristine beaches and secluded setting

These luxury resorts and boutique hotels in Phuket offer discerning travelers the ultimate indulgence with their upscale amenities, personalized service, and stunning locations. Whether you're seeking a tranquil beach retreat, a secluded rainforest hideaway, or a stylish urban escape, these properties promise a luxurious and unforgettable experience.

Unique Accommodation Experiences

Phuket offers a variety of unique accommodation experiences that promise to make your stay memorable. Here are some options for travelers seeking something out of the ordinary:

1. Overwater Bungalows:

- Experience the luxury of staying in overwater bungalows, reminiscent of the Maldives. These exclusive accommodations typically feature direct access to the sea, private decks with stunning views, and luxurious amenities.

2. Treehouse Villas:

- Stay in a treehouse villa nestled amidst the lush rainforest canopy. These eco-friendly accommodations offer a unique blend of luxury and nature, with panoramic views, open-air designs, and immersive jungle experiences.

3. Cliffside Retreats:

- Perched on dramatic cliffs overlooking the Andaman Sea, Cliffside retreats provide unparalleled views and seclusion. These exclusive accommodations offer privacy, luxury, and breathtaking sunsets from their elevated vantage points.

4. Private Pool Villas:

- Indulge in the ultimate luxury with a stay in a private pool villa. These exclusive retreats feature spacious villas with private infinity pools, lush gardens, and personalized service, offering a secluded oasis for relaxation and rejuvenation.

5. Luxury Yacht Stays:

- Experience the glamor of staying aboard a luxury yacht, exploring the azure waters of the Andaman Sea. These exclusive accommodations offer all the comforts of a five-star hotel, with the added bonus of breathtaking ocean views and unparalleled freedom to explore secluded coves and hidden beaches.

6. Boutique Heritage Hotels:

- Immerse yourself in Phuket's rich cultural heritage with a stay in a boutique heritage hotel. These charming properties are often restored colonial mansions or historic buildings, offering a glimpse into the island's past with modern comforts and personalized service.

7. Eco-friendly Glamping Sites:

- Experience the best of both worlds with a stay in an eco-friendly glamping site. These luxury tented accommodations blend outdoor adventure with comfort, offering stylish tents, plush furnishings, and eco-friendly amenities in pristine natural settings.

8. Floating Villas:

- Stay in a floating villa and enjoy the unique experience of living on the water. These exclusive accommodations feature spacious villas with panoramic views, private decks, and direct access to the sea, providing a tranquil and unforgettable retreat.

9. Cave Hotels:

- Explore the island's rugged landscape with a stay in a cave hotel. These unique accommodations are carved into the Cliffside or nestled within natural caves, offering a one-of-a-kind experience surrounded by stunning rock formations and ancient geological wonders.

10. Cultural Homestays:

- Immerse yourself in local culture with a stay in a traditional Thai homestay. Experience authentic hospitality, home-cooked meals, and cultural exchange with your hosts, gaining insight into the local way of life and creating lasting memories.

Whether you're seeking romance, adventure, or cultural immersion, these unique accommodation experiences in Phuket promise to elevate your stay and create unforgettable memories of your time in this tropical paradise.

Chapter 8

Nightlife and Entertainment

Phuket after Dark: Nightlife Hotspots

Phuket's nightlife scene is vibrant and diverse, offering something for everyone, from lively beach clubs and rooftop bars to bustling night markets and pulsating dance clubs. Here are some of the top nightlife hotspots in Phuket after dark:

1. Bangla Road (Patong Beach):

- Bangla Road is Phuket's most famous nightlife hub, known for its colorful neon lights, lively bars, and pulsating clubs. Stroll down this pedestrian street lined with bars, nightclubs, and street performers, and soak up the electric atmosphere.

2. Patong Beach Clubs:

- Experience beachfront partying at Patong's popular beach clubs, such as Paradise Beach Club, Café del Mar Phuket, and Illuzion Beach Club. Dance to the beats of international DJs, sip cocktails by the pool, and enjoy stunning sunset views.

3. Rooftop Bars:

- Enjoy panoramic views of the city and sea from Phuket's rooftop bars, such as Baba Nest at Sri Panwa, WOOBAR at W Phuket, and The 9th Floor. Sip on signature cocktails, relax in stylish lounges, and take in the glittering city lights.

4. Soi Seadragon (Patong Beach):

- Explore the lively nightlife of Soi Seadragon, a narrow street lined with go-go bars, beer bars, and nightclubs in the heart of Patong's entertainment district. Experience the vibrant nightlife scene and party until the early hours.

5. Phuket Night Markets:

- Discover Phuket's culinary delights and vibrant atmosphere at its night markets, such as Phuket Walking Street (Lard Yai) in Phuket Town, Chillva Market in Samkong, and Malin Plaza Patong. Sample street food, shop for souvenirs, and enjoy live music and cultural performances.

6. Simon Cabaret Show:

- Experience the glitz and glamour of Phuket's famous cabaret show at Simon Cabaret. Enjoy dazzling performances featuring extravagant costumes, elaborate sets, and talented performers showcasing Thailand's rich cultural heritage.

7. Live Music Venues:

- Enjoy live music performances at Phuket's bars and pubs, such as Red Hot Bar in Patong, Rock City in Phuket Town, and Laguna Beach Club in Bang Tao. Dance to the rhythm of live bands, sing along to your favorite songs, and enjoy a night of entertainment.

8. Old Phuket Town:

- Explore the charming streets of Old Phuket Town after dark and discover its eclectic mix of cafes, bars, and restaurants. Experience the local nightlife scene, sip cocktails in historic buildings, and admire the colorful Sino-Portuguese architecture.

9. Phuket Fantasea:

- Immerse yourself in Thailand's rich culture and mythology with a visit to Phuket Fantasea. Enjoy a spectacular evening of entertainment featuring Thai dance performances, elephant shows, and a grand buffet dinner in a themed village setting.

10. Bangla Boxing Stadium (Patong Beach):

- Experience the adrenaline-pumping excitement of Muay Thai boxing at Bangla Boxing Stadium in Patong. Watch professional fighters battle it out in the ring and cheer on your favorite contenders in this thrilling spectator sport.

From lively party streets to cultural shows and entertainment complexes, Phuket's nightlife offers endless opportunities for fun, excitement, and unforgettable experiences after dark. Whether you're seeking high-energy nightlife or laid-back entertainment, Phuket has something for everyone to enjoy after the sun sets.

Cultural Shows and Performances

Phuket, renowned for its vibrant culture, offers a plethora of captivating shows and performances that showcase the rich heritage of Thailand. Here are some must-see cultural shows and performances in Phuket:

1. Phuket Fantasea:

- Located in Kamala Beach, Phuket Fantasea is a cultural theme park renowned for its spectacular shows and entertainment. The main attraction is the "Fantasy of a Kingdom" show, which combines traditional Thai dance, music, and acrobatics with state-of-the-art special effects. Visitors can also enjoy a buffet dinner, carnival games, and shopping at the theme park.

2. Siam Niramit Phuket:

- Siam Niramit Phuket presents a grand theatrical production that showcases Thailand's rich history and cultural heritage. The show features elaborate sets, stunning costumes, and mesmerizing performances that depict scenes from Thai mythology, history, and folklore. Before the show, guests can explore the cultural village and enjoy traditional Thai activities.

3. Simon Cabaret Show:

- The Simon Cabaret Show is a world-famous transgender cabaret show located in Patong Beach. The show features glamorous performers in extravagant costumes, singing and dancing to a medley of popular songs. With its dazzling performances and vibrant atmosphere, the Simon Cabaret Show is a must-visit entertainment venue in Phuket.

4. Cultural Performances at Wat Chalong:

- Wat Chalong, one of the most important Buddhist temples in Phuket, often hosts cultural performances and ceremonies, especially during religious festivals and holidays. Visitors can witness traditional Thai dances, music, and rituals performed by local artists and monks, providing a glimpse into Thai religious and cultural traditions.

5. Thai Boxing (Muay Thai) Matches:

- Muay Thai, also known as Thai boxing, is Thailand's national sport and a significant aspect of its cultural heritage. Phuket hosts regular Muay Thai matches at various stadiums and venues, where visitors can witness thrilling bouts between skilled fighters. These matches offer an exciting and authentic cultural experience.

6. Traditional Thai Dance Performances:

- Many hotels, resorts, and cultural centers in Phuket offer traditional Thai dance performances for guests to enjoy. These performances typically include classical Thai dances such as the graceful "ram thai" or the dramatic "khon," showcasing intricate movements and elaborate costumes.

7. Street Performances at Night Markets:

- Phuket's night markets, such as Phuket Walking Street and Phuket Weekend Market, often feature street performers showcasing traditional Thai music, dance, and martial arts. These impromptu performances add to the vibrant atmosphere of the markets and provide entertainment for visitors.

Immerse yourself in the rich cultural tapestry of Thailand by experiencing these captivating shows and performances during your visit to Phuket. Each performance offers a unique opportunity to appreciate the beauty, diversity, and traditions of Thai culture.

Evening Markets and Street Food Delights

Phuket's evening markets are a paradise for food enthusiasts and bargain hunters alike, offering a vibrant atmosphere filled with tantalizing aromas, colorful stalls, and bustling crowds. Here are some evening markets and street food delights you shouldn't miss in Phuket:

1. Phuket Weekend Market (Naka Market):

- Located in Phuket Town, Phuket Weekend Market is the largest night market on the island, open every

Saturday and Sunday evening. Here you'll find a wide array of street food stalls offering local delicacies such as grilled seafood, pad Thai, mango sticky rice, and fresh fruit shakes. Don't forget to explore the market's other sections, where you can shop for clothing, accessories, souvenirs, and more.

2. Phuket Walking Street (Lard Yai):

- Phuket Walking Street, also known as Lard Yai, takes place every Sunday evening along Thalang Road in Phuket Old Town. This charming street market offers a cultural experience with its historical setting and traditional performances. Sample a variety of Thai street food favorites, including grilled meats, noodle dishes, Thai desserts, and savory snacks, as you stroll through the bustling market stalls.

3. Chillva Market:

- Chillva Market, located in Phuket Town, is a trendy night market popular among locals and tourists alike. Open every day, the market features an eclectic mix of food stalls, fashion boutiques, handmade crafts, and live music performances. Feast on a diverse range of street food options, from sushi burritos and gourmet burgers to Thai-style barbecue and sweet treats like crepes and ice cream rolls.

4. Karon Temple Market:

- Karon Temple Market is a lively night market held every Tuesday and Saturday evening at Wat Karon, near Karon Beach. This local market offers a more relaxed atmosphere compared to the larger markets in Phuket Town, with a focus on authentic Thai street food and snacks. Enjoy dishes such as grilled seafood, chicken satay, papaya salad, and coconut ice cream, as well as shopping for clothing, accessories, and souvenirs.

5. Patong Beach Road Night Market:

- Along Patong Beach Road, you'll find a bustling night market that comes alive after sunset. This market offers a mix of street food stalls, souvenir shops, and entertainment options, making it a popular spot for both locals and tourists. Indulge in Thai street food specialties like fried noodles, seafood skewers, grilled meats, and refreshing fruit shakes as you take in the lively atmosphere of Patong's famous nightlife district.

6. Rawai Seafood Market:

- If you're a seafood lover, don't miss the Rawai Seafood Market, located in the southern part of Phuket. This market offers an abundance of fresh seafood straight from the Andaman Sea, which you can have cooked to your liking at nearby restaurants. Feast on grilled prawns, steamed fish, crab curry, and other seafood delights while enjoying views of the ocean.

7. Banzaan Market:

- Banzaan Market is a large indoor market located in Patong Beach, offering a wide selection of fresh produce, meats, seafood, and ready-to-eat dishes. Visit the market in the evening to experience the bustling food court area, where you can sample a variety of Thai dishes such as pad Thai, green curry, stir-fried noodles, and mango sticky rice.

Explore Phuket's evening markets and street food delights to experience the island's vibrant culinary scene and indulge in delicious Thai flavors. Whether you're craving traditional Thai dishes, international cuisine, or sweet treats, you'll find an abundance of options to satisfy your taste buds at Phuket's lively night markets.

Chapter 9

Shopping and Souvenirs

Where to Shop in Phuket: Markets, Malls, and Boutiques

Phuket offers a diverse shopping experience, ranging from bustling markets and lively street stalls to modern shopping malls and boutique shops. Here are some of the best places to shop in Phuket:

Markets:

1. Phuket Weekend Market (Naka Market):

- Located in Phuket Town, this sprawling night market offers a wide range of goods, including clothing, accessories, electronics, souvenirs, and local handicrafts. It's also a great place to sample authentic Thai street food.

2. Phuket Walking Street (Lard Yai):

- Held every Sunday evening along Thalang Road in Phuket Old Town, this atmospheric street market features local vendors selling handmade crafts, clothing, antiques, and souvenirs. It's a great place to immerse yourself in Phuket's cultural heritage.

3. Chillva Market:

- Situated in Phuket Town, Chillva Market is known for its hip and trendy atmosphere. Here you'll find a variety of stalls selling fashion items, accessories, art, and handmade goods, as well as live music performances and food vendors serving up delicious street food.

4. Banana Walk:

- Located in Patong Beach, Banana Walk is a modern shopping complex featuring a mix of shops, restaurants, and entertainment options. You'll find a range of fashion boutiques, souvenir shops, and international brands, as well as a food court and movie theater.

Malls:

1. Jungceylon Shopping Mall:

- Situated in the heart of Patong Beach, Jungceylon is Phuket's largest shopping mall. It offers a wide selection of shops, including clothing stores, electronics outlets, beauty salons, and specialty shops. The mall also features a cinema, bowling alley, food court, and supermarket.

2. Central Festival Phuket:

- Located in Phuket Town, Central Festival Phuket is a modern shopping mall with a vast array of retail outlets, including international fashion brands, department stores, beauty stores, and home decor shops. The mall also houses a cinema complex, food court, and restaurants.

3. Premium Outlet Phuket:

- Situated on the Bypass Road, Premium Outlet Phuket is a shopping destination for bargain hunters. It offers discounted prices on a range of international and local brands, including clothing, footwear, accessories, and sportswear.

Boutiques:

1. Old Phuket Town:

- Explore the charming streets of Phuket Old Town, where you'll find an eclectic mix of boutique shops selling unique clothing, accessories, art, and souvenirs. The area is known for its Sino-Portuguese architecture and vibrant street art scene.

2. Surin Plaza:

- Located in Surin Beach, Surin Plaza is a boutique shopping complex catering to luxury shoppers. It offers a selection of high-end fashion boutiques, jewelry stores, art galleries, and home decor shops, as well as upscale restaurants and cafes.

3. Boat Avenue:

- Situated in Cherngtalay, Boat Avenue is a lifestyle and retail complex featuring boutique shops, gourmet food stores, cafes, and restaurants. It's a popular destination for upscale shopping and dining in Phuket.

From bustling markets to modern malls and chic boutiques, Phuket offers a diverse shopping experience that caters to every taste and budget. Whether you're looking for souvenirs, fashion items, or unique handicrafts, you'll find plenty of shopping opportunities to explore during your visit to the island.

Unique Souvenir Ideas

When it comes to souvenirs from Phuket, you'll find an array of unique and culturally rich items that capture the essence of this beautiful island. Here are some unique souvenir ideas to bring back home:

1. Handcrafted Thai Silk:

- Thai silk is renowned for its exquisite quality and vibrant colors. Look for scarves, shawls, or clothing made from traditional Thai silk, which make for elegant and luxurious souvenirs.

2. Wood Carvings and Sculptures:

- Phuket is home to skilled artisans who create intricate wood carvings and sculptures depicting Buddhist deities, animals, and traditional motifs. These handcrafted pieces make for beautiful and meaningful souvenirs.

3. Batik Fabric and Clothing:

- Batik is a traditional textile art form in Thailand, characterized by intricate patterns and vibrant colors.

Look for batik fabrics, clothing, or accessories such as bags and scarves as unique and stylish souvenirs.

4. Thai Herbal Spa Products:

- Treat yourself to a piece of Phuket's wellness culture by purchasing Thai herbal spa products such as massage oils, balms, soaps, and skincare products made from natural ingredients like lemongrass, coconut, and herbs.

5. Local Handicrafts and Home Decor:

- Explore the markets and boutiques in Phuket to discover a variety of local handicrafts and home decor items, including handwoven baskets, ceramic pottery, traditional masks, and decorative items made from bamboo or coconut shells.

6. Gemstones and Jewelry:

- Phuket is known for its gemstone industry, offering a wide selection of precious and semi-precious stones such as rubies, sapphires, and jade. Consider purchasing locally crafted jewelry pieces featuring these beautiful gemstones as a timeless souvenir.

7. Thai Cooking Ingredients and Spices:

- Bring the flavors of Thai cuisine back home by purchasing authentic Thai cooking ingredients and spices such as curry pastes, dried herbs, chili sauces, and coconut milk. You can also find beautifully packaged sets containing a variety of spices for gifting.

8. Traditional Thai Musical Instruments:

- Immerse yourself in Thai culture by purchasing traditional musical instruments such as bamboo flutes, xylophones, or drums. These unique souvenirs not only make for interesting decorative pieces but also provide a glimpse into Thailand's rich musical heritage.

9. Local Artwork and Paintings:

- Support local artists by purchasing original artwork or paintings inspired by Phuket's natural beauty, cultural landmarks, or everyday life scenes. Look for galleries or street artists selling their works in popular tourist areas.

10. Handmade Coconut Products:

- Coconut products are abundant in Phuket, and you can find a variety of handmade items such as coconut bowls, candles, soaps, and skincare products made from natural coconut ingredients. These eco-friendly souvenirs are both practical and sustainable.

Remember to shop responsibly and support local artisans and businesses when purchasing souvenirs in Phuket. These unique and culturally rich items will not only serve as reminders of your unforgettable trip but also contribute to the preservation of Phuket's rich heritage and traditions.

Bargaining Tips for a Successful Shopping Experience

Bargaining is a common practice in markets and street stalls in Phuket, and it's an essential skill for getting the best deals. Here are some bargaining tips to help you have a successful shopping experience:

1. Start with a Smile and Friendly Greeting:

- Approach the seller with a smile and a friendly greeting. Building rapport and showing respect can go a long way in establishing a positive bargaining atmosphere.

2. Do Your Research:

- Before you start bargaining, research the typical prices of the items you're interested in. Knowing the general price range will give you an idea of what is a fair price to pay.

3. Practice the "Walk Away" Technique:

- If the seller's initial price is too high, don't be afraid to walk away. Often, this can prompt the seller to lower their price to keep your business. However, be prepared to walk away for real if the seller doesn't meet your price.

4. Start with a Low Offer:

- Begin bargaining by offering a price that is significantly lower than what you're willing to pay. This gives you room to negotiate upwards while still getting a good deal.

5. Negotiate Incrementally:

- Bargain in small increments rather than making large jumps in your counteroffers. This keeps the negotiation process moving forward without offending the seller.

6. Be Polite and Respectful:

- Maintain a polite and respectful demeanor throughout the bargaining process. Avoid being aggressive or confrontational, as this can hinder your chances of getting a good deal.

7. Use Cash to Your Advantage:

- Paying with cash can sometimes give you more bargaining power, as sellers may be more willing to lower their prices for a cash sale.

8. Know When to Compromise:

- Be willing to compromise and meet the seller halfway if you're close to reaching a mutually acceptable price. Remember that bargaining is about finding a fair deal for both parties.

9. Be Prepared to Walk Away:

- If you're unable to agree on a price that satisfies both you and the seller, be prepared to walk away. There are usually plenty of other vendors selling similar items, so you may find a better deal elsewhere.

10. Enjoy the Experience:

- Bargaining can be a fun and engaging part of the shopping experience in Phuket. Approach it with a sense of adventure and enjoy the process of haggling for the best price.

By following these bargaining tips and maintaining a positive attitude, you can navigate the markets and street stalls of Phuket with confidence and come away with some great deals on souvenirs and gifts.

Chapter 10

Practical and Safety Tips

Money Matters: Currency, Tipping, and Bargaining

Here's a section on "Money Matters: Currency, Tipping, and Bargaining" for your Phuket travel guide:

Money Matters: Currency, Tipping, and Bargaining

Currency:

- The official currency of Thailand is the Thai Baht (THB). Notes come in denominations of 20, 50, 100, 500, and 1000 baht, while coins are available in 1, 2, 5, and 10 baht.

- It's advisable to exchange your currency to Thai Baht upon arrival in Phuket. Currency exchange counters are available at the airport, banks, hotels, and authorized exchange offices throughout the island.

Tipping:

- Tipping is not mandatory in Thailand but is appreciated for good service. In restaurants and cafes, a 10% service charge is often added to the bill, so tipping extra is not necessary but welcomed.

- For other services such as taxi rides, tour guides, and spa treatments, tipping is discretionary. A small tip of 20-50 baht is customary for good service.

- When tipping, it's best to give cash directly to the service provider rather than adding it to a credit card payment.

Bargaining:

- Bargaining is a common practice in markets, street stalls, and smaller shops in Phuket. It's expected that you negotiate prices, especially at markets and when purchasing items from street vendors.

- Start by offering a lower price than the seller's initial asking price, and be prepared to negotiate until you reach a mutually acceptable price.

- Keep the bargaining friendly and maintain a polite demeanor throughout the process. Remember that both parties should walk away feeling satisfied with the transaction.

- If you're not comfortable with bargaining, consider shopping at fixed-price stores or larger shopping malls where prices are more standardized.

Additional Tips:

- When using ATMs in Phuket, be aware of potential fees charged by your home bank and the ATM operator.

Look for ATMs that don't charge additional fees if possible.

- Carry small denominations of baht for convenience, especially when shopping at markets and street stalls where change may be limited.

- Keep your valuables and cash secure, especially in crowded areas and tourist hotspots. Consider using a money belt or secure pouch to store your money and important documents.

By understanding the local currency, tipping customs, and bargaining etiquette, you'll be better prepared to manage your finances and make the most of your shopping experiences in Phuket.

Staying Safe in Phuket: Dos and Don'ts

Here's a section on "Staying Safe in Phuket: Dos and Don'ts" for your travel guide:

Staying Safe in Phuket: Dos and Don'ts

Phuket is a beautiful destination with friendly locals and a vibrant atmosphere, but like any tourist destination, it's important to stay aware of your surroundings and take precautions to ensure a safe and enjoyable trip. Here are some dos and don'ts to help you stay safe in Phuket:

Dos:

1. Keep Your Valuables Secure:

- Keep your belongings secure at all times, especially in crowded areas and tourist hotspots. Consider using a money belt or secure bag to carry your valuables, and avoid displaying expensive items such as jewelry or electronics.

2. Stay Hydrated and Wear Sunscreen:

- Phuket has a tropical climate, so it's important to stay hydrated and protect yourself from the sun. Drink plenty of water throughout the day, especially if you're spending time outdoors, and use sunscreen with a high SPF to prevent sunburn.

3. Respect Local Customs and Culture:

- Familiarize yourself with Thai customs and etiquette, and show respect for the local culture. Dress modestly when visiting temples or religious sites, remove your shoes before entering someone's home or a temple, and avoid public displays of affection.

4. Use Licensed Transportation:

- Use licensed taxis, tuk-tuks, and transportation services to get around Phuket. Ensure that the meter is used in taxis, or negotiate a fare upfront. If using a motorcycle taxi, always wear a helmet and exercise caution on the roads.

5. Stay Aware of Scams:

- Be aware of common scams targeting tourists, such as overcharging for goods or services, fake tour operators, and gem scams. Use reputable tour operators and always confirm prices and details before making any payments.

6. Stay Informed about Weather Conditions:

- Phuket experiences monsoon seasons, so it's important to stay informed about weather conditions, especially if you're planning outdoor activities or water sports. Check weather forecasts regularly and be prepared for sudden changes in weather.

Don'ts:

1. Don't Drink Tap Water:

- Avoid drinking tap water in Phuket, as it may not be safe for consumption. Stick to bottled water or purified water from reputable sources to prevent waterborne illnesses.

2. Don't Engage in Illegal Activities:

- Avoid engaging in illegal activities such as drug possession or trafficking, as penalties in Thailand can be severe, including lengthy prison sentences or even the death penalty.

3. Don't Leave Your Belongings Unattended:

- Never leave your belongings unattended, especially on beaches or in crowded areas. Keep an eye on your belongings at all times to prevent theft or loss.

4. Don't Get Involved in Altercations:

- Avoid getting involved in altercations or disputes with locals or other travelers. Stay calm and walk away from any confrontations to prevent escalation.

5. Don't Ignore Safety Warnings:

- Pay attention to safety warnings and advisories, especially during monsoon season or in areas prone to natural disasters such as tsunamis. Follow the advice of local authorities and take appropriate precautions.

6. Don't Forget Travel Insurance:

- Make sure you have comprehensive travel insurance that covers medical emergencies, trip cancellations, and other unforeseen events. It's better to be prepared for any eventuality while traveling in Phuket.

By following these dos and don'ts, you can help ensure a safe and enjoyable experience during your visit to Phuket. Remember to stay vigilant, use common sense, and take precautions to protect yourself and your belongings while exploring this beautiful destination.

Health and Medical Services

Here's a section on "Health and Medical Services" for your travel guide:

Health and Medical Services

Medical Facilities:

- Phuket is equipped with modern medical facilities and hospitals that cater to both locals and tourists. Some of the reputable hospitals on the island include Bangkok Hospital Phuket, Phuket International Hospital, and Vachira Phuket Hospital.

Emergency Services:

- In case of a medical emergency, dial 1669 for ambulance services in Phuket. These services are available 24/7 and can provide prompt assistance in transporting patients to the nearest hospital.

Pharmacies:

- Pharmacies, known as "drugstores" in Thailand, are readily available in Phuket. Look for pharmacies marked with a green cross symbol. They stock a wide range of medications, over-the-counter drugs, and basic medical supplies. Some pharmacies are open 24 hours.

Medical Insurance:

- It's highly recommended to have comprehensive travel insurance that includes coverage for medical emergencies while visiting Phuket. Check with your insurance provider to ensure that your policy covers medical expenses, hospitalization, and medical evacuation if necessary.

Travel Health Tips:

- Prior to traveling to Phuket, consider visiting a healthcare professional for any necessary vaccinations or medications. Common recommendations include vaccines for hepatitis A and B, typhoid, and tetanus.

- Stay hydrated by drinking bottled water and avoid consuming tap water, ice cubes, and uncooked foods from street vendors to prevent gastrointestinal issues.

- Protect yourself from mosquito bites by using insect repellent, wearing long sleeves and pants, and staying in accommodations with screened windows or air conditioning, especially during dawn and dusk when mosquitoes are most active.

- Practice safe sun protection measures by wearing sunscreen with a high SPF, seeking shade during peak sun hours, and wearing sunglasses and a hat to protect your eyes and face from UV radiation.

Traveler's Health Advisory:

- Stay informed about any health advisories or travel warnings issued by your home country's health department or the World Health Organization (WHO) regarding Phuket. This may include updates on infectious diseases, environmental hazards, or other health-related concerns.

Language Barrier:

- While many healthcare professionals in Phuket speak English, there may still be language barriers, especially in rural areas. Consider carrying a basic medical phrasebook or translation app to communicate essential medical information if needed.

By familiarizing yourself with the available medical services, taking necessary health precautions, and being prepared for potential medical emergencies, you can ensure a safe and healthy trip to Phuket.

Emergency Contact Information

Here's a section on "Emergency Contact Information" for your travel guide:

Emergency Contact Information

Police:

- Emergency: 191

- Tourist Police: 1155 (English-speaking officers available)

Medical Emergencies:

- Ambulance: 1669

Bangkok Hospital Phuket:

- Address: 2/1 Hongyok Utis Road, Muang District, Phuket 83000

- Phone: +66 76 254 425

Phuket International Hospital:

- Address: 44 Chalermprakiat Ror 9 Road, Muang District, Phuket 83000

- Phone: +66 76 249 400

Vachira Phuket Hospital:

- Address: 353 Yaowarat Road, Taladyai, Muang District, Phuket 83000

- Phone: +66 76 361 234

Fire Department:

- Emergency: 199

Tourist Assistance:

- Tourist Assistance Center: +66 76 327 100 (Phuket Tourist Police Headquarters)

- Tourist Police Hotline: 1155

Embassy and Consulate Information:

United States Embassy Bangkok:

- Address: 95 Wireless Road, Lumpini, Pathumwan, Bangkok 10330

- Phone: +66 2 205 4000

Embassy of Canada Bangkok:

- Address: 15th Floor, Abdulrahim Place, 990 Rama IV, Bangrak, Bangkok 10500

- Phone: +66 2 636 0540

Embassy of the United Kingdom Bangkok:

- Address: 14 Wireless Road, Lumpini, Pathumwan, Bangkok 10330

- Phone: +66 2 305 8333

Australian Embassy Bangkok:

- Address: 181 Wireless Road, Lumpini, Pathumwan, Bangkok 10330

- Phone: +66 2 344 6300

Other Useful Contacts:

- Tourist Information Center: +66 76 212 213

- Airport Information: +66 76 327 230

Language Barrier:

- While many emergency services personnel and tourist assistance centers in Phuket speak English, there may still be language barriers. Consider carrying a translation app or phrasebook for essential communication during emergencies.

Ensure travelers have access to emergency contacts and are prepared to use them in case of need during their visit to Phuket.

Chapter 11

Itineraries

1-week Itinerary

Here's a suggested 1-week itinerary for a memorable trip to Phuket:

Day 1: Arrival and Relaxation

- Arrive in Phuket and check into your accommodation.

- Spend the day relaxing on one of Phuket's beautiful beaches, such as Patong Beach or Kata Beach.

- Enjoy a leisurely dinner at a beachfront restaurant and watch the sunset over the Andaman Sea.

Day 2: Island Hopping Adventure

- Embark on an island-hopping tour to explore the stunning islands and marine life around Phuket.

- Visit popular destinations like Phi Phi Islands, James Bond Island, or Similan Islands for snorkeling, swimming, and sunbathing.

- Return to Phuket in the evening and dine at a seafood restaurant in Rawai or Patong Beach.

Day 3: Cultural Exploration

- Discover the rich cultural heritage of Phuket by visiting Wat Chalong, the largest Buddhist temple on the island.

- Explore Phuket Old Town and admire the Sino-Portuguese architecture, vibrant street art, and local markets.

- Attend a traditional Thai cooking class to learn how to prepare authentic Thai dishes.

- In the evening, watch a cultural show or traditional Thai dance performance.

Day 4: Adventure and Nature

- Embark on an adrenaline-pumping adventure with activities such as zip-lining, ATV riding, or jungle trekking in Phuket's lush rainforest.

- Visit Phuket Elephant Sanctuary or Gibbon Rehabilitation Project to learn about wildlife conservation efforts in Thailand.

- Relax and unwind with a traditional Thai massage or spa treatment in the afternoon.

Day 5: Beach Day and Water Sports

- Spend another day soaking up the sun on Phuket's beaches or indulge in water sports activities such as parasailing, jet skiing, or paddleboarding.

- Explore the underwater world with a snorkeling or diving excursion to coral reefs and marine sanctuaries.

- Enjoy a beachside barbecue dinner with fresh seafood and cocktails.

Day 6: Shopping and Sightseeing

- Shop for souvenirs and gifts at Phuket's bustling markets, such as Phuket Weekend Market or Jungceylon Shopping Mall.

- Visit Big Buddha, an iconic landmark overlooking the island, and enjoy panoramic views of Phuket from the hilltop.

- Take a sunset cruise around Phang Nga Bay or enjoy a romantic dinner cruise along the coast.

Day 7: Departure

- Take a morning stroll on the beach and savor your last moments in Phuket.

- Check out of your accommodation and transfer to Phuket International Airport for your departure flight.

- Depart Phuket with unforgettable memories of your island paradise vacation.

Adjust the itinerary based on your interests, preferences, and available time to make the most of your 1-week stay in Phuket.

Exciting Day Trips from Phuket

Exploring the surrounding islands and attractions near Phuket makes for exciting day trips filled with adventure and natural beauty. Here's a suggested itinerary for day trips from Phuket:

Day 1: Phi Phi Islands

- Start your day early and head to the pier to catch a speedboat or ferry to the Phi Phi Islands.

- Explore the stunning landscapes of Phi Phi Leh, including Maya Bay (made famous by the movie "The Beach"), Loh Samah Bay, and Viking Cave.

- Enjoy snorkeling in the crystal-clear waters and marvel at the colorful marine life and coral reefs.

- Visit Phi Phi Don for lunch and relax on the beautiful beaches, such as Long Beach or Monkey Beach.

- Return to Phuket in the late afternoon and unwind at your hotel or explore Patong Beach's vibrant nightlife.

Day 2: James Bond Island and Phang Nga Bay

- Embark on a day tour to Phang Nga Bay, famous for its limestone karsts and emerald-green waters.

- Visit James Bond Island (Khao Phing Kan), known for its starring role in the James Bond movie "The Man with the Golden Gun."

- Explore the hidden caves and lagoons of the bay by kayak or long-tail boat.

- Stop by the floating village of Koh Panyee and learn about the local way of life.

- Enjoy a seafood lunch on the floating restaurants or at a nearby island.

- Return to Phuket in the evening and relax after a day of adventure.

Day 3: Similan Islands

- Join a day trip or speedboat tour to the Similan Islands, a renowned diving and snorkeling destination.

- Explore the underwater paradise of the Similan Marine National Park, home to vibrant coral reefs, diverse marine life, and clear waters.

- Enjoy snorkeling or diving at famous sites like Donald Duck Bay, Christmas Point, and Elephant Head Rock.

- Relax on the pristine beaches of the islands and soak up the sun.

- Return to Phuket in the late afternoon and treat yourself to a relaxing spa session or dinner at a beachfront restaurant.

Day 4: Phuket Old Town and Cultural Tour

- Spend the day exploring the rich history and culture of Phuket Old Town.

- Wander through the charming streets lined with colorful Sino-Portuguese buildings and vibrant street art.

- Visit historical landmarks such as Thalang Road, Soi Romanee, and the Phuket Thai Hua Museum.

- Discover local markets, boutique shops, and art galleries showcasing traditional and contemporary Thai art.

- Enjoy a traditional Thai lunch at a local restaurant and savor the flavors of Phuket's cuisine.

- In the evening, catch a cultural show or traditional dance performance at one of the theaters in Phuket Town.

Day 5: Elephant Sanctuary and Khao Sok National Park

- Embark on a day trip to an ethical elephant sanctuary in the nearby region.

- Spend the morning interacting with rescued elephants in a natural environment, feeding them, and observing their behavior.

- Learn about elephant conservation efforts and the importance of responsible tourism.

- Enjoy a delicious Thai lunch at the sanctuary or nearby restaurant.

- In the afternoon, head to Khao Sok National Park for a jungle trekking adventure.

- Explore the lush rainforests, limestone mountains, and hidden waterfalls of Khao Sok on a guided hike.

- Return to Phuket in the evening and unwind with a leisurely dinner at a local restaurant or beachside cafe.

Day 6: Coral Island (Koh Hae)

- Take a speedboat or ferry to Coral Island (Koh Hae), located just a short distance from Phuket.

- Spend the day snorkeling in the crystal-clear waters and exploring the vibrant coral reefs teeming with marine life.

- Enjoy water activities such as parasailing, jet skiing, and banana boat rides.

- Relax on the pristine white sandy beaches and soak up the tropical sunshine.

- Indulge in a beachfront barbecue lunch with fresh seafood and local delicacies.

- Return to Phuket in the late afternoon and enjoy a sunset cocktail at a beach bar overlooking the Andaman Sea.

Day 7: Relaxation and Beach Day

- Dedicate your last day in Phuket to relaxation and leisure.

- Choose your favorite beach, whether it's Patong Beach for its lively atmosphere, Kata Beach for its picturesque scenery, or Surin Beach for its tranquil vibes.

- Spend the day swimming, sunbathing, and enjoying water sports activities.

- Treat yourself to a beachfront massage or spa treatment for the ultimate relaxation experience.

- As the sun sets, take a leisurely stroll along the beach and savor the magical moments of your time in Phuket.

- In the evening, enjoy a farewell dinner at a seaside restaurant, reminiscing about your unforgettable adventures in Phuket.

With these exciting day trip options, you can experience the best of Phuket's natural beauty, cultural heritage, and outdoor adventures during your stay on the island. Each day trip offers a unique opportunity to explore different aspects of Phuket and create lasting memories of your vacation in this tropical paradise.

Exploring Nearby Islands

Exploring nearby islands from Phuket is an adventure-filled experience that offers breathtaking landscapes, pristine beaches, and vibrant marine life. Here's a suggested itinerary for exploring nearby islands:

Day 1: Phi Phi Islands

- Start your day early and embark on a speedboat or ferry to the Phi Phi Islands.

- Explore the iconic sights of Phi Phi Leh, including Maya Bay (made famous by the movie "The Beach"), Loh Samah Bay, and Viking Cave.

- Enjoy snorkeling in the crystal-clear waters and discover colorful coral reefs and marine life.

- Visit Phi Phi Don for lunch and relax on the stunning beaches, such as Long Beach or Monkey Beach.

- Return to Phuket in the late afternoon and unwind at your hotel or explore the vibrant nightlife of Patong Beach.

Day 2: James Bond Island and Phang Nga Bay

- Join a day tour to Phang Nga Bay, known for its limestone karsts and emerald-green waters.

- Visit James Bond Island (Khao Phing Kan), famous for its appearance in the James Bond movie "The Man with the Golden Gun."

- Explore the hidden caves and lagoons of the bay by kayak or long-tail boat.

- Stop at the floating village of Koh Panyee and learn about the local way of life.

- Enjoy a seafood lunch on the floating restaurants or at a nearby island.

- Return to Phuket in the evening and relax after a day of adventure.

Day 3: Similan Islands

- Embark on a day trip or speedboat tour to the Similan Islands, renowned for their pristine beaches and vibrant underwater life.

- Explore the stunning coral reefs and marine biodiversity through snorkeling or scuba diving.

- Visit iconic dive sites such as Donald Duck Bay, Christmas Point, and Elephant Head Rock.

- Relax on the picturesque beaches and soak up the sun's rays.

- Return to Phuket in the late afternoon and treat yourself to a relaxing evening at a beachfront restaurant.

Day 4: Coral Island (Koh Hae)

- Take a short speedboat ride to Coral Island (Koh Hae), located just off the coast of Phuket.

- Spend the day snorkeling in the crystal-clear waters and discovering colorful coral reefs and tropical fish.

- Enjoy water sports activities such as parasailing, jet skiing, and banana boat rides.

- Relax on the pristine white sandy beaches and soak up the tropical sunshine.

- Indulge in a beachside lunch with fresh seafood and local delicacies.

- Return to Phuket in the late afternoon and unwind after a day of island exploration.

Day 5: Racha Islands (Racha Yai and Racha Noi)

- Join a day trip to the Racha Islands, known for their stunning beaches and excellent diving and snorkeling opportunities.

- Explore the white sandy beaches and turquoise waters of Racha Yai, perfect for swimming and sunbathing.

- Discover vibrant coral reefs and marine life while snorkeling or scuba diving around Racha Noi.

- Enjoy a delicious seafood lunch at a beachfront restaurant on one of the islands.

- Return to Phuket in the late afternoon and relax after a day of island hopping.

Day 6: Koh Yao Yai and Koh Yao Noi

- Take a scenic boat ride to the tranquil islands of Koh Yao Yai and Koh Yao Noi, located in Phang Nga Bay.

- Explore the laid-back atmosphere of the islands and discover pristine beaches, lush jungles, and traditional villages.

- Enjoy activities such as kayaking, cycling, or hiking to explore the natural beauty of the islands.

- Visit local markets and shops to experience the authentic island lifestyle and purchase souvenirs.

- Relax on the beach and savor a delicious seafood dinner at a beachfront restaurant.

- Return to Phuket in the evening and reminisce about your island adventure.

Day 7: Relaxation and Leisure

- Dedicate your last day in Phuket to relaxation and leisure.

- Choose your favorite beach on Phuket, such as Patong Beach, Kata Beach, or Surin Beach, and spend the day swimming, sunbathing, and enjoying water sports activities.

- Treat yourself to a beachfront massage or spa treatment for the ultimate relaxation experience.

- As the sun sets, take a leisurely stroll along the beach and savor the magical moments of your island exploration.

- In the evening, enjoy a farewell dinner at a seaside restaurant, reminiscing about your unforgettable adventures in Phuket.

With these exciting island exploration options, you can experience the natural beauty, cultural heritage, and outdoor adventures of the nearby islands during your stay in Phuket. Each day trip offers a unique opportunity to discover the diverse landscapes and marine life of the Andaman Sea and create lasting memories of your island getaway.

Adventure Activities beyond Phuket

Venturing beyond Phuket opens up a world of exhilarating adventure activities, from jungle trekking to zip-lining and more. Here's a suggested itinerary for adventure activities beyond Phuket:

Day 1: Khao Sok National Park

- Depart early from Phuket and travel to Khao Sok National Park, located approximately 2-3 hours away.

- Embark on a guided jungle trekking adventure through the lush rainforest of Khao Sok, home to diverse flora and fauna.

- Explore stunning limestone formations, hidden waterfalls, and serene rivers.

- Enjoy a thrilling bamboo rafting or canoeing experience along the Sok River, surrounded by towering limestone cliffs.

- Spend the night in a rustic jungle bungalow or eco-lodge, immersing yourself in the natural beauty of Khao Sok.

Day 2: Cheow Lan Lake

- Wake up to the sounds of the jungle and enjoy breakfast overlooking the breathtaking scenery of Khao Sok.

- Head to Cheow Lan Lake, also known as Ratchaprapha Dam, for a day of exploration on the water.

- Take a long-tail boat ride to explore the tranquil lake, surrounded by towering limestone karsts and lush greenery.

- Visit stunning attractions such as Guilin Rock, Nam Talu Cave, and Coral Cave.

- Enjoy swimming, kayaking, or paddleboarding in the crystal-clear waters of the lake.

- Spend the night in a floating bungalow or tent raft on Cheow Lan Lake, experiencing the unique charm of this remote wilderness.

Day 3: Flying Hanuman Zipline Adventure

- Return to Phuket and embark on a thrilling zipline adventure at Flying Hanuman.

- Soar through the treetops on a series of ziplines, sky bridges, and abseiling lines, offering panoramic views of the jungle canopy below.

- Navigate through the lush jungle terrain and encounter various obstacles and challenges along the way.

- Enjoy a delicious Thai lunch amidst the natural beauty of the jungle.

- Relax and unwind in the afternoon, or explore other nearby attractions in Phuket such as beaches or cultural sites.

Day 4: ATV Adventure in Phang Nga

- Join an ATV (All-Terrain Vehicle) adventure tour in Phang Nga province, located northeast of Phuket.

- Ride through rugged terrain, dense forests, and muddy trails on your ATV, experiencing the thrill of off-road adventure.

- Explore hidden trails, remote villages, and scenic viewpoints overlooking the stunning landscapes of Phang Nga.

- Visit local attractions such as waterfalls, temples, and caves, learning about the region's natural and cultural heritage.

- Enjoy a delicious Thai lunch at a local restaurant before returning to Phuket in the late afternoon.

Day 5: White Water Rafting on Ton Pariwat

- Experience the adrenaline rush of white water rafting on the Ton Pariwat River in Phang Nga province.

- Join a guided rafting tour and navigate through thrilling rapids, twists, and turns along the river.

- Enjoy the scenic beauty of the surrounding jungle and limestone cliffs as you paddle downstream.

- Stop for a refreshing swim in the river and explore nearby waterfalls and natural pools.

- Conclude your rafting adventure with a hearty Thai lunch before returning to Phuket in the afternoon.

Day 6: Bungee Jumping or Skydiving

- For the ultimate adrenaline-pumping experience, consider bungee jumping or skydiving in Phuket.

- Head to a reputable adventure sports center and take the leap from a towering platform or soar through the sky with a tandem skydiving jump.

- Feel the rush of adrenaline as you freefall through the air and enjoy breathtaking views of the coastline below.

- Capture the unforgettable moment with photos or videos to commemorate your daring adventure.

- Relax and unwind in the evening, reflecting on your thrilling experiences beyond Phuket.

Day 7: Beach Day and Relaxation

- Dedicate your last day in Phuket to relaxation and leisure.

- Choose your favorite beach on Phuket, such as Patong Beach, Kata Beach, or Surin Beach, and spend the day swimming, sunbathing, and enjoying water sports activities.

- Treat yourself to a beachfront massage or spa treatment for the ultimate relaxation experience.

- As the sun sets, take a leisurely stroll along the beach and savor the magical moments of your adventure-filled trip.

- In the evening, enjoy a farewell dinner at a seaside restaurant, reminiscing about your unforgettable experiences beyond Phuket.

With these thrilling adventure activities beyond Phuket, you can push your limits, explore remote wilderness areas, and create lasting memories of your journey in Thailand. Each day offers a unique opportunity to experience the thrill of adventure and immerse yourself in the natural beauty of the region.

Conclusion

As your journey in Phuket comes to an end, take a moment to reflect on the memories you've created, the adventures you've experienced, and the beauty of this tropical paradise. From pristine beaches and lush rainforests to vibrant culture and thrilling activities, Phuket offers a wealth of experiences that captivate the senses and leave a lasting impression.

Whether you've explored the iconic sights of Phi Phi Islands, delved into the rich history of Phuket Old Town, or embarked on adrenaline-pumping adventures beyond the island, your time in Phuket has been filled with discovery and wonder.

As you bid farewell to Phuket, remember to carry with you the warmth of the sun on your skin, the taste of authentic Thai cuisine, and the smiles of the friendly locals you've encountered along the way. Cherish the moments of relaxation, exhilaration, and connection that have enriched your journey and sparked your sense of wanderlust.

As you venture back to your everyday life, may the memories of Phuket continue to inspire you and remind you of the beauty and magic that awaits in the world. Whether you return to Phuket in the future or explore new destinations afar, may your travels be filled with joy, adventure, and endless discovery.

Thank you for choosing Phuket as your destination, and until we meet again, may your travels be filled with endless adventures and unforgettable experiences.

Safe travels and farewell from the beautiful island of Phuket!

Printed in Great Britain
by Amazon